waking up
In Corporate America
The Seven Secrets That Opened My Eyes

Published by Advantage, Charleston, South Carolina.
Member of Advantage Media Group.

ADVANTAGE is a registered trademark and the Advantage colophon is a trademark of Advantage Media Group, Inc.

Printed in the United States of America.

Cover photo courtesy of Nic Oatridge

ISBN: 978-1-59932-055-7
LCCN: 2007939585

Most Advantage Media Group titles are available at special quantity discounts for bulk purchases for sales promotions, premiums, fundraising, and educational use. Special versions or book excerpts can also be created to fit specific needs.

For more information, please write: Special Markets, Advantage Media Group, P.O. Box 272, Charleston, SC 29402 or call 1.866.775.1696.

waking up

IN CORPORATE AMERICA

THE SEVEN SECRETS THAT OPENED MY EYES

Eric Pennington

Advantage™

Table of Contents

Preface | 7

SECRET 1:
Be Authentic | 11

SECRET 2:
Live a Life of Influence | 23

SECRET 3:
Don't Chase Success | 37

SECRET 4:
Beware of the Evil
Number Seventeen | 53

SECRET 5:
Water Cooler Conversations | 67

SECRET 6:
Embrace Reality | 81

SECRET 7:
Brand You | 99

Acknowledgements | 117

FOR THOSE WAKING UP...

Preface

When the idea for this book came to me, I at first ignored it. This was due to my tendency to over analyze things and put them away for another day. However, I believe there is a major untapped resource out there in Corporate America. That resource is you. I want to help you move from just surviving to thriving. That is why I could not ignore the call to write this book.

My motivation is to speak to you where you are—the corporate citizen, or maybe slave. I was there; I spent almost twenty years charting the treacherous waters where many things just didn't make sense.

If you are like me, you think there has to be more to a career than stock options, promotions, and retirement. It took me a while, but I discovered that corporate life did mean more than the aforementioned. I found work is a vehicle designed to move us to that place where we know and are known. I know that may sound strange, but it's true.

You see, we've made the mistake of thinking career and work success was the aim. But I'm here to tell you it's about life success—not at the expense of career, but to the enhancement of it. Some might say this is a contradiction, and these people are probably ninety-five percent of the senior managers out there today.

I don't claim to be a genius or visionary, but after participating in about two million meetings (yes, I've lived to tell), I know there is something terribly wrong out there. I think you agree with me. Matter of fact, I know you do because I've talked to you. Much of this book was born out of frank and sobering conversations with a wide range of corporate soldiers. The looks in the eyes, the pauses, and the sighs point to a workplace experience we all share.

This book is not designed to insult or indict Corporate America. At the end of the day, we all have to work, and some of us were destined to do that within a corporate structure. I believe the majority of senior managers and their fellow executives are well intentioned. I think they want to do the right thing, but like you, they can't seem to make sense of this thing called work. Consequently, the problem is we were never meant to make sense of work; we were supposed to make sense of life and then work would take care of itself.

I've compiled seven principles (or secrets) that have worked in my life and career. I'm sure there are many more out there, but I look at these as the seven most important. Additionally, they represent real world experience. The people referenced within are people I know (though some of their names have been changed to protect the innocent and guilty) or have met in a one-time encounter. Their stories are a part of what makes the book and journey relevant. Relevancy is vital in discovering breakthroughs that last.

This book will not solve every issue, but I'm confident it will bring clarity and direction. I've set out to help you discover what you were designed to do. Abraham Maslo, in his "Hierarchy of Needs," says self-actualization is a human being's number one need. I agree!

God created 6.8 billion people, so you might wonder where you fit in. He gave us each unique DNA and a unique story to tell. We spend so much of our time in this thing called work, so shouldn't we live it with meaning? After spending almost twenty years in Corporate America, I think most folks want that sense of purpose. Unfortunately, many people in organizations are not developed, and over the years they grow cynical and jaded. For the life of me, I don't understand why organizations don't grow their people. Organizations are so fixated on earnings and expenses they've forgotten what gives them the fuel (people) for their growth. I don't expect I will change your CEO's mind, but maybe I can help you realize that your life is the most important pursuit.

SECRET 1
Be Authentic

*Authentic leaders realize that power flows
through them, not from them.*

--Ken Blanchard

Some years ago, Rick Williams, a wise mentor and friend, advised me to not let the corporation define me. He also advised me to be the authentic person I was designed to be. Those words still reverberate in my mind. Many pundits might think healthcare or career advancement would be the greatest issues people face in the workplace. But I believe being authentic is possibly the biggest issue/struggle facing people inside Corporate America today.

Definitions will determine the level of our authenticity. This is true for all people, whether they know it or not. I call those that don't know it the "working dead." In order to define ourselves properly, we must begin with authenticity in mind. Authentic motivations, authentic thoughts, and authentic dreams are essential. If we're not authentic leaders, then we're counter-genuine leaders. It's a daunting challenge, but we must find a way to develop authenticity and bury insincerity.

THE LAND OF AUTHENTIC

Authentic behaviors occur when we are willing to make sacrifices and trust our gut. If you've been caught in the vacuum of positioning, a place where everything is staged for the audience (usually your boss), then this might be difficult to embrace. Be willing to communicate your authentic opinions and actions as if life depended on it. In other words, take risks. Put something on the line! Consider risk as an entrance exam into authenticity.

Another exciting occurrence in the place called "authentic" is a sense of destiny. The first installment of the movie *The Matrix* communicates this brilliantly. The character Neo is on a path of destiny. The journey is long and risk-filled, but he presses on. As you may remember, he isn't entirely sure of himself throughout the film. But in the final showdown, he awakens to who he truly is. Neo realizes he has the gift, and he embraces it. We've all been given the gift of authenticity. Unfortunately, very few ever accept and embrace it.

If senior managers rose to the level of authentic, we'd have more people willing to be themselves. Organizations would then have environments full of honest two-way communication. They would be beautiful states where ideas, obstacles, and opportunities are laid out on the table. They would be places of trust. Such organizations would ultimately be the high performers.

Don't allow yourself to stay in a place where positioning is the norm, you will start to become as you behold. Examine the health of the enterprise carefully. Signpost up ahead: senior managers rarely wake up where corporate sleeping is condoned. Follow your vision and leave the organization if you need to.

THE POWER OF AUTHENTICITY

Let's now explore how we move to practicing authentic behaviors. First, remember that authentic influence applies to everyone, whether you are an entry-level receptionist or the CEO. Far too often, we buy into the lie that this mind-set is exclusive to high-level executives. I remember a time when an associate engaged me in a robust discussion about authentic leadership. He had a variety of opinions about the subject. Jack was an inquisitive guy, but we had rarely spoken about such things. He had a history of not taking no for an answer. He also questioned everything, with a strong opinion to boot. As we began the conversation, I passionately spoke of the importance of authenticity. He really wanted to agree, however it was obvious he didn't grasp the concept. More than likely, his experiences reflected what most of us have endured. I told him the essence of my concept was diversity, the kind of diversity where everyone's voice (not their skin color) really matters. After our spirited discussion, he realized I truly wanted the work group to be originals and not replicas. This was strange science because he'd been asked to be a duplicate under so many past leaders.

Allowing people to be authentic gave me a reputation of being a little over the top, but my team was always the better for it. Think about it, do we really want an environment where fakes are the norm? Most people I've led want the opportunity to be themselves (while doing their best in their area of expertise). Organizations blow it when they don't encourage authentic behaviors. It's the authentic leaders who produce the greatest results. Name one organization where fakes carried the day? You would probably need to check the bankruptcy filings to find them. When you evaluate an environment, work or otherwise, make sure it embraces authentic behaviors—behaviors like honest communication and courage under fire.

THE PROBLEM WITH COUNTER-GENUINE INFLUENCE

I've had many examples in my career of what counter-genuine influence looks like (in managers and non-managers alike). About ten years ago, I worked for just such a leader. Bill really didn't like people, but he continually pursued managing them. He wanted the paycheck and power that managing provided. Bill didn't get the connection between the love of people and influencing.

As someone who reported to him, I felt no love. There were many days where he struggled even to say hello. I sometimes wondered if I was a phantom. Because he wasn't an engaging man, he didn't make the attempt to connect with me. Despite this, I found myself many times wanting to ask him why he pursued leading people. Looking back, that kind of question would have led to my firing.

Ironically, Bill lit up like a Christmas tree whenever the group president came around. He was definitely a charter member of the ChapStick Club of America. Needless to say, my gut says he was lost in a maze that so many leaders are. You know the place, a place where the idea (I want the privilege of power, not the responsibility) of something is better than the reality.

By the way, your organization is possibly an enabler of leaders like Bill. Every counter-genuine leader needs a sponsor. In the name of fear and greed, Corporate America acts as this willing sponsor.

Counter-genuine leaders wear many faces and play many roles. Of course, the roles change depending on what the scene calls for, but one of my favorites involves the "I really care about you" conversation. These conversations usually happen when senior managers return from seminars or workshops where motivational speakers inject them with some good insights. However, they're not connected to living out what they have learned.

I once had a division president ask me how my family was doing. I almost fell out of my chair. Now keep in mind this was at a company picnic. I was rather shocked because she had never, in the three years I worked there, asked me about my family. She seemed sincere, but ironically, she never asked me again.

Counter-genuine leaders do just enough to play a role, but no more. Most counter-genuine leaders are so inwardly focused, they fail to see that most people can spot insincerity a mile away. Here's a news flash for all the senior managers in the room: your people know and see more than you think.

The agendas used by counter-genuine leaders include climbing the wrong corporate ladder, micro managing those they lead, denying responsibility when things go wrong, and pure hungering for power. In their book, *Leadership on the Line,* Ronald Heifetz and Marty Linsky give some wise insights about power. "Power can become an end itself, displacing your attention to organizational purposes. An inflated sense of self-importance can breed self-deception and dysfunctional dependencies."

What causes leaders to run from authentic behaviors and motivations? Most counter-genuine leaders have developed patterns and habits that can reach as far back as childhood. Authenticity implies uniqueness, which our society does not embrace. Just look around you…conformity is more the norm. Don't misunderstand me, we all need boundaries, but not to the point where it chokes out our unique self.

I'll give you an example of someone I managed for many years. Her name was Jane. Jane was a different thinker. I knew this from the moment I met her. To her, Corporate America was a breeding ground for compromise and conformity. In many ways, she felt the work environment was a place where people could feel loved. Jane was a feeling-driven person, and she was definitely a corporate casualty.

Her different thinking was considered a threat inside the organization. We worked in an environment where marching to management's drum was a form of career protection. Typically, conservative companies frown upon independent thought (even when they say they welcome it). Our group needed refreshment, and I needed her help to turn the enterprise around. One of the ways to do this was to seek out leaders who wanted to be authentic, even if they had never been given the opportunity before. Jane was intrigued by my overtures, but it was clear to me it would take time for her to trust my intentions.

As the weeks passed, I began to understand the wounds Jane possessed. She was somewhat defensive and tended to be suspicious of corporate leaders. This made perfect sense because most of the leaders she worked with were counter-genuine. We talked a lot, and as the months passed, she began to discover her own authentic style. That style was always there, but the organization wasn't producing the right kind of conditions for authenticity. Most of her experiences were with leaders who thought leadership meant power and privilege. So Jane did as many do; she withdrew from authentic behaviors.

Trust is a key component of any relationship, especially inside a conservative organization. Our workplace wasn't the easiest place for two people to build trust. But once we were able to connect on that level, we benefited from a couple significant by-products of trusting each other. First, I gained a lot as the leader of the group because a different point of view was given freely. Second, Jane experienced growth because she felt free to be herself. This is the essence of empowerment. I'll never forget her thanking me for showing her that it was okay to be authentic. What an honor it was to receive such a compliment.

The journey to authentic leadership is full of difficult and scary turns. Many give up because no one is there to spur them on. It is sad to think of all of the potential wasted. It's ironic that being you (being authentic) is discouraged, while posing is considered a norm. Jane gave me great inspiration regarding the importance of changing for the sake of authenticity.

WHAT EVER HAPPENED TO DREAMING?

Come with me now to a time when you were a kid. Imagine you were interested in things the other kids were not. (For some, this will require less imagination than others.) Maybe you liked a certain type of music that others did not or you played a sport that wasn't popular. More than likely, you were made fun of or shunned. You probably began feeling embarrassed and isolated. If you didn't have someone to tell you it was okay to be different, you more than likely buried your interest. Certainly, embracing and exploring your interest would have been the best route to take.

The bottom line is being authentic starts with self-examination. Bill George, in his book *Authentic Leadership,* recounts the following experience around self-examination and authenticity, "My commitment to myself was to be the same person at home, at work, in the community, and in church. During this time, Penny was a great reality check, challenging me when she observed me behaving differently in social settings, for example, and talking to me about how I could change. This was not easy. It took years before I could make these interior walls disappear and let people in every aspect of my life know who I really was." Are you ready for this? Don't be afraid. The dream is you, and you are the dream.

THE ROAD MAP TO AUTHENTICITY

If we're going to find the big rocks of authenticity inside ourselves, then we need a place where we can be alone—a quiet place for reflection where we can think. I've found my home office and Caribou Coffee to be excellent places for quiet reflection.

Author and speaker John Maxwell recommends setting an appointment for reflective time. Follow John's advice! It works! I have applied the appointment-setting concept for some time, and I'm the better for it.

The busy life you live will scream that you don't have time for reflection, but you must ignore that voice. In one of the work groups I led, there was a lady who put me to the test on this subject. Sandy was someone who would say, "I just don't have time." She followed that statement by giving me a laundry list of her obligations. I asked her once if she wanted her daughter to be like her. Of course, her reply was yes. I then exhorted her to slow down and model the art of reflection so her daughter would learn from her example at an early age.

Sadly, so many of us are moving at such a clip we find slowing down to be for the birds. Think about it, how much time do you spend watching television or playing golf? Those activities are not inherently bad, but comparatively speaking, they don't have near the personal value of self-discovery.

Once you've mapped out time and found a quiet place, bring something to write with so you can capture the points on paper. The written word has tremendous power, and you'll be better able to remember it. Capture the things that are uniquely you, and narrow the list to no more than five items. I struggled with this one, but my best advisors told me when you get beyond five, you start to lose focus. Losing focus will create confusion and doubt, which are the archenemies of your authentic self.

Now that you have your big five, ask yourself a few questions. For example, would I do this thing/action/endeavor for free? Can I literally see myself doing it? Does it excite me like nothing else in life? Questions like these are designed to make sure you are connecting to your unique self. You'll probably hear the negative voices telling you how silly you are, how it won't work, how other people will perceive it, and the list goes on. Your inner voice, the one God gave you, is the only voice that matters in this exercise.

Now is the time for a life mentor. I have what is sometimes referred to as a "mentoring constellation." This is a group of people who are my trusted advisors and allies. This group includes my wife, Eileen, and three other people I count on for counsel and feedback. A life-mentor will help keep you accountable and can encourage you along a dangerous path. (Life is a dangerous pursuit.) This mentor should be someone whom you can trust, someone who is not impressed by you, and someone who is willing to speak truth. Believe it or not, some organizations—GE, Northrop Grumman, and Dow Chemical, to name a few—are starting to embrace mentoring in a formal way. They believe it's important for the wisdom and knowledge of senior executives to be passed on to new leaders in the enterprise. These practices are part of a strategy to deal with the "brain drain" anticipated in Corporate America when a vast number of senior leaders, who are baby boomers, retire. I commend these organizations for embracing the principles of mentoring. Maybe more organizations will latch on to this powerful interaction.

MAKING A BREAKTHROUGH

I have a good friend who once warned me he had a keen nose for self-deception. There were times I didn't like him being so discerning, but some of my greatest breakthroughs came from his frankness. Breakthroughs are things you need. Most people have forgotten life is supposed to be a growth event. In our obsession with business, we've let corporations steal the true meaning of growth. How many organizations do you know that are really growing? Maybe you can name a handful, but more than likely your list will be short. I can't say enough about how important people like my friend Eric are. In the journey to authenticity you need mentors like this. They will challenge you, they will encourage you, and they will be there to wipe the tears you cry-seen and unseen. In the end, growth is born out of relationships like this. Don't miss the opportunity to engage with the greatness of others!

THE BIG THWARTERS

The last step in the process is the great and challenging opportunity of living out what you've learned. I consider this to be the most difficult part of authentic leadership. We all are bombarded with temptations, hardships, and general difficulties that can act as big thwarters of our best intentions. For example, on the temptation front, you can count on times where you will be asked to agree for the sake of group thought. To go in another direction would lead to isolation and scorn. I can tell you from experience that firestorm you face doesn't compare to the alternative of compromise. When you sit in meetings, like I did, with the president of the company, it is very tempting to waiver. When we waiver, it's usually rooted in our unwillingness to risk. We've been taught we shouldn't listen to that still small voice…not to believe our authentic self is worthwhile. So in turn, we listen and conform to the voice of the division head.

This is why going through these processes will build your confidence. You'll need that confidence to be strong when the heat is on. Paying a heavy price for standing firm is hard, but the long-term rewards are out of this world. Author and speaker Jackie Freiberg calls this gutsy leadership.

Unfortunately, most of us were never guided or taught how to handle the big thwarters. I believe it's a matter of building daily habits. Go look for opportunities to be confident. Speak up in that next meeting. Resolve conflict that you used to avoid. Be fully alive!

Some of you are thinking, what if I get in trouble? What if I get fired? Now hear this, any organization that doesn't value guts and confidence is probably already dead. They just haven't had the burial yet. These organizations have ceased to be relevant and are more than likely soon to go out of business or be sold to a competitor.

Giving in to fear is the worst thing we can do when facing these types of situations. You must remember that success follows those who are willing to be true to themselves (authentic).

I once attended a senior management meeting where an announcement was made regarding one of my associates, Tom. This gentleman made the decision to leave our organization after only working for one week. A company who had been pursuing him returned to the table with an offer too good to pass up.

I will confess I was disappointed in Tom's decision, but I believe I would have done the same thing if I were in his shoes. After the announcement was made, many in the room began hurling an expletive that I won't print here. One of those individuals was the president of the company. It would have been easy to just ignore the comments, but I felt compelled to defend Tom. The Golden Rule applies here.

Needless to say, I didn't win any fans that day. Most of the individuals in that room were looking for validation. Don't forget; most organizations value conformity and duplication.

Dead enterprises believe, naively, that they can control change (often manifested in a warped sense of reality). Therefore, they hire senior and mid-level executives who are managers rather than leaders.

In this case, the managers were deeply insecure and unprofessional. By taking a stand that day, I won the future with my integrity intact. People who understand that God made them for a purpose and destiny find ways to summon courage.

SECRET 2
Live a Life of Influence

Everyone has influence; the test is in how we use it.

--Eric Pennington

Over the years, I've found many people underestimate the power of influence. Because they can't see it with their eyes, they tend to write influence off. Look at influence as a kind of "cause and effect." For example, if a manager fails to schedule a performance appraisal, the employee would feel unimportant. The manager may be well in-tentioned (and unorganized), but her influence is one of inequity and indifference. This leads to failed leadership, which we could substitute for failed influence.

As we look at our cultural landscape, it's obvious that influence carries a great deal of weight. Take, for example, the corporate scan-dals occurring inside a number of organizations. Whether you look at United Healthcare, Dell, or Qwest, you are sure to see signs of self-serving influence. This type of ethics crisis is an indicator of how im-portant influence is.

Isn't it interesting that many leadership experts equate influence with leadership? Based on my experiences in many different settings, influence and leadership are one and the same. Corporations and non-profits would do well to take influence more seriously. The cost (in human and financial terms) is obviously huge. Just ask the former employees of Enron. Everyone carries the power of influence. The real test is in how that influence is used.

OUR COMPASS HAS US OFF COURSE

How did we get to a place where we underestimate the power of influence? Our corporate compass has us off course. It has us pointed in a direction that confines influence to those who hold formal leadership positions. This elitist approach has left many "informal" leaders in a position where they neither see nor feel they have voices in the arena of influence. Consequently, these people never exercise the greatness found within them.

Corporate America fosters the elitist approach to influence by its worship of celebrity. Ironically, some of our greatest leaders are those who don't appear in the latest issue of *Fortune*. These people exist under the corporate radar. They're people like Samantha, who consistently answered the phones in our work group with a smile on her face. She always seemed to want to influence people in a positive way. I can't think of one time when she didn't succeed at being that wonderful first impression. She happened to be our frontline receptionist. I don't think she ever made a lot of money or received any big awards, but she was one of the most important people in the company.

Author Ken Blanchard notes that the most important people in a company are those closest to the customer. Sadly, a majority of corporate executives miss this truth and run the red light of reality. You see, it's people like Samantha who are starving for enlightened executives to recognize their strengths. Such executives use their influence to say "you first" and "I'll support you." I've seen the tremendous power in treating members of my work group this way. People truly come alive when their managers put them first.

In the corporate world, middle managers believe leadership is a privilege and/or entitlement. That type of mindset produces a very dysfunctional culture. (And you thought your extended family had issues?) These types of corporate cultures are full of obsessions, bitterness, and insecurity. Sound familiar?

The damage done to people (and their organizations) due to dysfunctional management mindsets is evident in a number of significant ways. Just look at the high turnover rates inside many businesses. It's not uncommon to find organizations running at a fifteen percent turnover rate, and that number doesn't even account for the damaged people who have chosen to stay in the organizations.

Sexual harassment, racial discrimination, and gender bias are all issues that arise out of a failure to recognize the universality of influence. The true cost of these approaches will not be fully felt until Corporate America experiences the coming worker shortage. That will be a time when many will discover the connection between influence and leadership. With all the baby boomers retiring in the next decade, things are going to get very interesting in the realm of leadership and influence. The smartest organizations, though, are those that view influence as a very powerful force to be reckoned with.

WAKING UP

In order to fully understand where we want to be, we need to look back and connect the dots. It personally took me over ten years to awaken from the slumber that is self-serving influence. I use those words because they best describe my former disposition. Like many other leaders, I found myself making mistakes I wasn't conscious of. Discovering that influence and leadership are one and the same, I lived out the "cause and effect" of influence.

There were many experiences in my early years that shaped my pursuit of success. The majority of them were self-centered in nature. I thought the more I achieved and amassed, the more I would be okay in the eyes of others. The approval of others was essential. The message I heard from the corporate culture was relax and enjoy the ride. I understand now how misleading that message was.

While I was running this race (or should I say rat race?), I found I was also running from myself. The way I was managing my life was an accident waiting to happen. I would periodically hit the wall and wonder where I was. During those periods, I always thought there must be more to life than scaling the corporate mountain.

During these early years, only my wife knew of my loneliness and pain. I feel, like many, my wife is my best friend, and she has an uncanny level of intuition. I'm so thankful she didn't give up on me. Work wasn't the only place where my self-serving approach existed. The behaviors could also be found in my family, my church, and my friendships. Self-serving leaders are never compartmentalized.

The path out of focusing on me alone began in the year 2000. I experienced hardship in my career, finances, and health, including the loss of a child. It seemed as if God decided it was time for real change, and by the end of that year, I was broken.

Saying I was ready for change would've been an understatement. My game of pretense was over…I woke up and gradually my true self came into focus. I felt sort of like the addict who finally realizes he has a problem. The journey was long, but eventually others truly came to matter more than my agenda. The self-serving gave way to an others-first approach. I started to value feedback, encouragement, and coaching from many whom I historically ignored. Whether it was my wife or my pastor, I started listening.

When you come to the end of yourself, you begin to realize you're better because of the people in your life. We were never intended to walk our unique paths alone.

As you might have figured out, the journey also requires that each person face a "crucible." Often this is an event that will define our paths (very much like my year 2000 journey). Until we go into a valley, regardless of the level or intensity, we won't see what matters most. Warren Bennis and Robert Thomas, in their great book, *Geeks and Geezers,* have this to say regarding the power of crucibles; "whether imposed or sought out, crucibles are places where essential questions are asked: Who am I? Who could I be? Who should I be? How should I relate to the world outside myself? These are always places of reflection, but they are typically places where one transcends narrow self-regard and reflects on the self in relation to others. They are often places where one becomes increasingly aware of his or her connectedness."

INFLUENCE IN THE WORKPLACE

When we think about how influence plays itself out in the workplace, the issue of people leaving an organization is crucial. There are some compelling reasons behind why people leave organizations. Pay scale, "old" environments, and no inspiration are a few that come to mind. The Gallup Organization says sixty-five percent of turnover in Corporate America is directly related to the relationship a person has with his or her manager. In other words, most people "fire their managers."

In 2004, I made moves in my career that fit just that scenario. My "manager," who happened to be the president of the company, crossed an ethical line that compelled me to confront him directly. We were asked to participate in a "confidential" survey. My wife warned me about these so-called confidential surveys. In the back of my mind, I knew I was taking some risk, but I wanted to help shape and improve our organization. When the findings were given to senior management, it didn't take my manager very long to confront me.

Jack was the type of manager who believed his power gave him authority he didn't truly possess. When he asked me about my "confidential" opinions, I told him he should begin searching for my replacement. The look on his face said it all. He seemed genuinely shocked. I think he believed I was connected to the organization at birth. Surely, I would never entertain sticking to my core values.

Ironically, Jack and I had spoken many times in the past about where I stood on a number of fronts. But he, like so many senior leaders, only paid lip service to the things that didn't directly impact him. So when I took a stand, he didn't know what to say or do.

Sadly, there were other situations prior to this one that reflected poorly on Jack's judgment, but I knew I was doing the right thing in taking a stand. Senior leaders who are self-serving don't have a clue about whom or what they lead. To the organization's credit, they removed Jack shortly after my encounter.

BEYOND THE CORPORATE MACHINE

Our personal lives can illustrate how influence applies to areas not often thought of. A great example for me is marriage, a place where transparency and commitment go hand-in-hand. I've been blissfully married for fourteen years, but the early years of my marriage were a time where, again, I discovered how much influence I had without even knowing it. Call it youth or stupidity; either way, it was a blind bet.

If you were to talk to my wife, Eileen, she probably would tell you the first three years of our marriage were not the greatest. Quite frankly, divorce wouldn't have been so strange a decision. In marriage, the first season is often one of the toughest. It's a time where laying down your weapon is a tough prospect, let alone all the agendas.

As you might imagine, I brought my agenda; my wants; and, worst of all, my habits to the relationship. Whether it was watching television in excess or paying lip service to Eileen's opinions and recommendations, this type of influencing left Eileen lonely. She was a new bride and found herself isolated and brokenhearted.

I had no idea about how important giving and serving was. Oh sure, I read the books and went to the seminars. We even took a premarital class designed to prepare us for the give-and-take of marriage. But I still thought my way was the best way. Foolishly, I was rigid and thought that Eileen needed to change. I was wrong. Starting to see the negative side of influence? Everyone lives a life of influence; it's just a matter of what type of influence you're dispensing.

About five years into our marriage, I began to see that the majority of the issues were with me. I started to realize that I had a lot of influence, and I'd better make some changes or Eileen would be gone. The thought of that was heart wrenching. Eileen was, and is, the most important person in my life. Love is too limiting a word to describe how I feel about her.

I started to embrace the type of habits that would make my influence meaningful and sustaining. For example, I learned the art of admitting, and saying, I was wrong. Thankfully, Eileen could see the authenticity behind my words and actions. This was key because words and actions are only as good as their connection.

As our relationship grew, we both realized we were a team and not opponents. I matured to a point where my side was her side. We moved to looking at things as "one," not as two different camps. I look back now and see how the power of influence almost ruined me and then saved me.

THE BEST INFLUENCE WE CAN LIVE

Organizations can change for the better when influence is used to grow people. The world changes when influence is used to grow people. People begin to be inspired and energized. They use the conditions and environments to reconnect with themselves in addition to reconnecting with the outside world. This is a type of reconnection that opens up possibilities. The possibilities amount to something greater than any individual. Self-serving people need not apply.

It's a powerful reality when you experience a leader who desires to use his or her influence to help others. Your best organizations actively recruit and develop such leaders; they don't look at influence as an accidental encounter. This type of entity realizes that accidents happen ten percent of the time; the other ninety percent is about choices. Best-in-class organizations are purposeful about the beneficial use of influence. They formalize it by initiating programs, encouraging behaviors, and overseeing execution. Sadly, low-performing organizations sit idly by wondering, "What's all the fuss about."

We can't wait for corporations, churches, or associations to make the use of positive influence a reality. Seize the opportunity and become more purposeful about how you use your influence.

A key advisor, Laura, once told me how she had to take ownership of her influence. Laura was always confident, but her career wasn't stimulating, and most of her superiors didn't seem interested in her aspirations. This led to a variety of dead-end streets. She would master a certain discipline and quickly become bored. Managers would ask her to be involved in projects that quickly became uninspiring. Laura realized it was time to take her rightful place at the table of influence. After years of letting others control the impact of her influence, she knew her life was ebbing away. She came to a crossroads (as we all do) and chose to follow a path of authentic influence. Laura was comfortable with the fear, the doubt, and the uncertainty that come with this type of move.

There is always a price for these types of decisions. As you aspire to live a life of influence, it will bring you rejection from middle management, friends, and even family. This happens because most individuals who live a life of influence are visionary. Visionary people speak about the unseen, which can make people very uncomfortable. But those who understand the mystical and powerful nature of influence will welcome it like water on a hot summer day. There's no way around it; if you embrace influence, you will be misunderstood.

Laura knew it wasn't going to be easy, but she understood that many times it's about an act of our will. Laura has never looked back. I had the privilege of watching her grow over many years. Not often do you get to see this type of transformation. It was a blessing indeed. Laura went on to succeed in many arenas (education, business, and non-profits) that our culture recognizes as great. But if you were to ask her today about the choice to embrace her unique influence, she would say it was all about the "choice"—the choice to not be a victim, the choice to see a better future, and the choice to be who she was meant to be. Without a doubt, Laura is truly remarkable.

STARTING POINTS

So how do we start living a life of influence? The first step in the transformation is recognizing the power behind our personal influence, or leadership. Everyone has some level of influence. We either use it for the benefit of others, or we use it for our own gain. The latter creates the insidious self-serving model.

Have you identified the people and organizations in your sphere of influence? I suggest you take an inventory so you can begin to completely measure your impact. Once your inventory is complete, you must evaluate specifically how your influence affected the outcomes with each person or organization. In the career arena, identify your daily, weekly, and monthly impacts—places where the organization looks squarely to you for the end product. For instance, what were the outcomes of a presentation given to your work group? What resulted from your interactions in a meeting? Away from the office, how did an exchange with your daughter about the best part of her school day conclude? The answers to these questions will be revealing. Often these are events where you're solely accountable for the result.

When I led a sales group some years ago, I was transforming into a servant leader. At that time, one of the people in my sphere of influence was John. John would say my support helped him become the top seller in our division and one of the top salespeople in the entire company. He was a type A person and emotional, too. These two traits can be lethal. Despite his personality type, I admired him and wanted to see him grow to his fullest potential. As I became more of a servant leader, I began doing what servants do...using my influence to serve. Of course, I set proper boundaries (accountability, balance, and honest feedback) around my servant leadership. Within those boundaries, I did everything I could to help John in his pursuits. Sharing in his successes would never have happened if a different model had been applied. My influence on John was significant.

If you're a person of excellence or someone learning to be one, then imagine what your job function would be like if you were gone. Apply this technique to all facets of your life. Think about it; excellence is rare, and people with knowledge of their influence are rarer still. My guess would be you have more value than you think. Once you realize the extent of your value write it down! These words will have tremendous power for you and, most importantly, for the people around you. These will be the words that land on your resume, in your biography, and in the elevator speech to the managing director. The importance of life mentors shines through here. They will be the sounding board to help you make sense of what comes from your brainstorm.

From this point in your journey, you should begin to seek out greater opportunities to influence the world around you. It doesn't matter if you want to pursue volunteering at a homeless shelter or becoming a part of the management team in your organization. People of influence want to make a difference, and they're also called to a life of growth.

Practically speaking, the world is starving for those who desire to make a greater impact. Far too often, we underestimate how many pockets of influence there are to impact. Could your family gain value from consistent on-purpose encouragement on a daily basis? I bet that answer would be a resounding yes. Could your work group gain value from someone willing to find creative ways to introduce new products? I bet your division manager would be ecstatic over that possibility. As you can see, there are numerous ways to live a life of influence.

THE SERVE IN SERVING

My friend Steve Hopkins once told me, "You're not ready to lead until you're ready to serve." Influence with a servant's heart is the most powerful form of leadership.

Sir Ernest Shackleton exemplified this idea in his quest to cross Antarctica in 1915. When the expedition ran aground (literally), Shackleton displayed a type of servanthood that is, to this day, inspiring. He thought only of his men's welfare. He went to the heart of influence by sacrificing his dream for the survival of those who followed him.

Does today's corporate culture rise to Shackleton's example? I think not. The idea of serving is too mystical for most to embrace. It's so rarely lived out that we don't see the value in practicing the art. We've fallen for the idea that being number one is most important. This would be the twenty-first century trinity: me, myself, and I. The leader who is focused on him-or herself would be our norm today.

In some ways, you might understand why we're so self-serving inside Corporate America. Most senior managers are taught early on that it's about their future, their money, their position, their promotion, and the list goes on.

The breeding ground (high school and college) for corporate folk fosters this self-serving approach as well. These institutions tell individuals their achievements will deliver certain outcomes. Many times, outcomes are based on theory alone. In our minds, being in charge, making lots of money, or acquiring prestige can lull us into believing those outcomes are reality. Is it a surprise that most under-graduate and graduate programs are pursued to enhance economic status?

If we're honest, we might concede that our society's issue with ethics relates directly to a self-serving mindset. Just pick up any edition of the *Wall Street Journal* to see the impact on Corporate America. You may have even experienced unethical behavior in your own work world. We've been seriously damaged by those who seek their own interests first.

I have led many middle-level managers who were taught the nonsensical mantra of self-service. Our relationships began with my vision on how we would go about accomplishing our mission. I would tell them we were the least important people in the enterprise. Things would come to a screeching halt, at least for them; I was used to the air bags deploying.

Great was the opportunity to bring my team back to reality—a reality where the most important people were those closest to the customer. Being the least of many does not mean you will never make money, rise in your level of influence, or build a great career. But what it does mean is you will do and have these things after you put others first.

Does this concept strike you as counterintuitive? Some of the greatest ideas are that way. Take the path of knowing you're not truly successful until you help someone else be successful.

AS WE THINK

Warning: here comes the warning label, or at least a few words of caution. If you've never lived a life of influence, there will be some twists in the road ahead. We're now going to look at the impact of how we think. If you're already on the path, then take this as great reinforcement.

You must take two important steps to overcome roadblocks you're likely to set up for yourself on your path to greatness. First, you will need to confront your approach to thinking. Our thought life is one of the clearest indicators of where we are in our pursuit of an epic life.

Here's a very important question to ask: Do you hear voices? Really, do you hear voices? These voices might make toxic comments like "your opinion will be made fun of" or "you're not smart enough." These voices are the seeds behind poor thinking. I spent way too many years allowing those voices to convince me my ideas didn't matter. They took control of my identity and, therefore, my influence.

What would your life be like if you ignored these poisonous assessments? You would have a life marked by influence and greatness. So start today; take the second step to overcoming the roadblocks and ignore the poison. Every thought dedicated to changing the way you think will go a long way in neutralizing the negative voices.

It won't be easy, but your unique greatness requires these steps. Our thinking reflects our ability to see the power we have. Influence is waiting for us to awaken and seize that which was given to us at the start.

SECRET 3
Don't Chase Success

*The world is full of people who mistake
net worth for self-worth.*

--Author Unknown

One of the most ruinous preoccupations today is success. It's a type of success defined in the wrong way and one that leaves you wanting more. Like a cat chasing its own tail, so it is with our culture and success.

Go to any magazine, television show, or book and you'll get a number of messages about success. For example, a glossy spread in your favorite periodical may imply that buying a certain brand of car will raise your status. A 30-second spot on the tube might tell you you'll be seen as prestigious if you attend a certain university. A chapter in the latest best seller from the business section is likely to explain how to impress your boss with well-timed ideas.

You may even work for an organization that preaches a "success doctrine" that amounts to furthering the organization's objectives at the cost of your full life. Sound familiar? In moments of clarity, most would say they've bought into this idea. Some might even admit to giving up on any other idea of success.

Like wine, success unto itself is not a bad thing. Also like wine, success can become destructive when you use it for the wrong reasons, such as to take away sadness. In the end, success was designed (yes, designed) to serve.

What would your world look like if you didn't chase success? Would you have less stress? Would you be more content with life? The answer is an obvious yes to me, but you may doubt that. As mystical as it might sound, success is waiting for us to "give the command." Sadly, if you don't give that command success will. When this happens, you will begin the chase. Some have run this race their entire lives and never figured out that it was all for naught.

True success should produce new frontiers of growth and risk— places where your heart beats faster and the desire to win is evident. When you consider these frontiers (action), you can't get around the implication of dynamism. Dynamic people chart courses all their own. They have a sense that they were made to do something great. Something inside them tells them that life was not meant to be a spectator sport. Conversely, static people are looking for the path of least resistance. They dream of early retirement and a pension that will last for the remainder of their days. No danger and minimal risk are what they seek.

How about you? Are you willing to go against the tide? It is the tide that most accept and even embrace. The tide will decide your fate if you let it.

People who have stopped chasing success are to be marveled at. They've decided to accept that there is a tide, but it wasn't designed to rule them. They are the rare souls who experience success in a way that we all long for. People who have stopped chasing success have a sense that the story has already been written. They are defined by destiny.

THE GOOD LIFE

The true successful life begins by focusing on what makes you come alive and pursuing that end. This is the place that defines why and what you were made for. It's been calling your name forever, but maybe you've ignored the voice. In today's culture, you might be considered a nut for talking about voices. Ignoring your voice is easy today. Not many are comfortable with being looked upon as a nutcase. Most of us are looking to fit in.

As you pursue the vision of your destiny, you'll find little time for fretting about money, position, and power. You'll develop what my friend and mentor, Rick Williams, calls a non-anxious presence. You'll start to understand that there are greater things than a Lexus. You won't be fazed by the clothes on your back. People pursing their vision know what matters and what will take care of itself. They know their mortgage doesn't need the attention known as fretting. Know this, these folks are very successful in many categories. What's inspiring is, they know the things of success are by-products of pursuing vision.

A TOUGH ROAD

I wish I could end the chapter now by saying the rest will be a walk in the park. But I can't, and you might know why. When you give up the chase of success, you're choosing a tough road. Our culture doesn't buy the idea of no fear or worry. Fear and worry are common denominators for many people.

Thus, we have the great pursuit of success. The world says somehow we'll be better when we have. Having can be in the form of people, possessions, and the like. Have you ever asked why we can't seem to get enough of these things?

Chasing success is a true fool's game. Believe me; I have scars from that game. At one point, I thought continued performance and achievement in a corporate setting would be everything.

The corporate world is ill equipped to provide that kind of security. If you're not careful, something as important as your family will take a backseat. You'll find yourself completely identified with the wrong landscape, once again, confusing what success really means.

Fortunately waking up is an option. You'd better do it early rather than late, because the older you get, the more challenging it is to change. I learned this from my good friend Eric, who gave me a wonderful gift of advice, which I'll never forget. He told me my time was in front of me, so I'd better take the risk now. It was as if he knew we have only a certain number of chances in life.

I was thirty-nine years old at the time Eric spoke those words. What also struck me was the warning he gave me along with his advice. The danger of fifty he called it. He said this is what happens when you reach a point in life where risk becomes too risky. Many baby boomers are hiding behind success to mask the surrender that has already occurred when there is no more dreaming, no authentic leadership, and no consideration of a legacy left.

We need to embrace risk and not give up. Don't make the fatal mistake of burying a brilliant destiny in the ground. A longer view is more daunting, but it is the way in which we build a great life. Do you really want to chase something that continually leaves you wanting more?

WHY DO WE CHASE SUCCESS?

People tend to chase success for three main reasons: fear, self-worth, and selfishness. The order of these reasons can vary, but the result is the same. Success becomes a matter of identity. In many ways we see ourselves in the mirror of success-or failure. Ever met someone who seems to have everything, but can never relax? Ever met someone that checks email at their kid's baseball game? If you have, then you've witnessed someone chasing success.

OK, I'M AFRAID

There's enough research to prove that we are afraid. Let's face it; we're all human. It has been said fear is the driver—the driver of those things that paralyze us and keep us up at night. A significant number of Americans are controlled by their fears: fear of change, fear of the unknown, and the list goes on.

Margaret Thatcher was able to win power in England because she knew how to provide strength in the face of people's fears. She knew for a prosperous society to function, people needed to sense that all is well. She met that need with approach and actions.

Whatever the fear is, it can create an almost obsession for instant results and gratification. When we are able to get things fast, we feel more secure. Therein produces the quandary, our fear pushes us to impatience and rash decision making. It also convinces us we have more control than we truly have.

Consider the Generation Xers; they are consistent in their belief that knowledge is all that matters. Experience is a subjective element. They are a group that constantly watches the clock. The trait of impatience is never a good thing. Sadly, this is not an issue confined to a certain age group or generational culture. The demon of impatience lurks everywhere.

My friend Don happens to be a Generation X guy. He is pursuing success like there's no tomorrow. Virtually every conversation we have is rooted in his desire to "get there." He wants to be the CEO, the owner, the one to watch. He drips ambition and frustration. Frustration you wonder? Things are not moving fast enough, and therein lies the problem.

Organizations (especially corporations) love people like Don. A committed follower is worth three of the working dead. People who will do anything to succeed, will do anything to succeed.

Don has told me he needs to be patient, but he also confesses that he can't rest. Though he's never told me, I bet the lure of all the things money can buy has charmed him. He doesn't value slowing down. There's always that fear he might miss the next big thing. As Don chases success, he always finds himself one deal away from hitting it big.

Don is building wealth, but he's not building a wealthy life. What he's missing is the big picture and a clear vision of the future. Don would do well to let success catch up.

THE WORTH GAME

Another complex issue facing us is the temptation to connect our self-worth with our net worth. This is the, sometimes unconscious, habit of feeling good about yourself only when you possess things, people, power, etc. It's like trying to fill a vacuum that always returns to empty, and it is no respecter of persons.

More than a few times, I have fallen into the trap of the worth game. Let me tell you, *trap* is the right word for it! You find yourself in this maddening cycle that doesn't seem to end. Most of the time, you have to hit a wall or lose something and/or someone to get out of it.

Maybe you've played the worth game before. Maybe you're playing it now. What has you running? Is it the power of a corner office? Or maybe you're racing after a bigger bonus? It really doesn't matter which one.

Are you uncomfortable now? If you are, you are probably waking up. You sense there is no amount of whatever you're chasing to equal to your true worth. God made things this way for a reason.

I once worked with a gentleman named Max. Max was a very insecure man. He couldn't see life as complete unless he had a certain amount of money or some type of position that legitimized him as a person. Like many of us, when he was a child, he didn't hear from his adult influences that he was "okay."

A number of people in your formative years can cast a broad shadow. Whether it's your parents or another caregiver, you will be impacted. As crazy as it may sound, hearing someone with great influence in your life validate you as a human being is powerful. Some never overcome the absence of these words, and the void stays with them all their lives.

Max was obviously in a race—a race with himself. As the years unfurled, he always had a new venture or new position. These were stage props for a lonely existence. I can vividly remember him asking once how he was supposed to behave as an executive. He didn't quite believe he belonged in the world he strived so hard to find. This was the height of Max's loneliness. He was chasing success at his own expense.

Over time, Max began to understand that no amount of money or possessions could validate his self-worth. Max likened this understanding to growing up. As he deepened his relationship with God and started to seek council from friends and family, he started to awaken. Max today is much more at peace. He's not perfect, but he has a much healthier outlook. However, I'm sure he would tell you it is a daily battle to keep his perspective in line with reality.

ME, MYSELF, AND I

The last area of concern is selfishness. This type of selfishness resembles someone who, in public and private, cannot allow anyone or anything else to come first. Selfish behavior isn't changed easily because most of us are wired to be selfish at some level. At the right level, selfishness is healthy. A healthy form of selfishness would be blocking out an hour a week for you to think and plan. However, if selfishness gets out of control, someone's going to get hurt. There is nothing worse than meeting, living, or working with someone who thinks it's all about him or her. Remember, if it's all about you, then it can never be about anyone else. Selfish attitudes are perpetuated by living in a culture obsessed with success.

There are thousands of messages coming at us every day telling us it is about us. Things like weight loss, retirement savings, and career advancement are all promoted with "do it for you" slogans. The secondary message is, "You'll be more attractive/comfortable/powerful than the other guy." We don't like to admit to it, but we do like to think we've got it made—first. It's easy to forget that eventually all the stuff that happens to "other people" can happen to us. But if that reality is never mentioned (except for the fine print) we can easily believe the other guy has it worse off.

Thinking about others first seems unnatural...almost burdensome in practice. We mistakenly believe if we don't get ours, we'll be left out in the cold. Though counter-intuitive, nothing could be further from the truth. Just think of families, churches, and volunteer organizations that not only speak about others first, but actually reflect it in their daily actions. Marveling at how remarkable they are is a waste of time. Go put the concept into practice and you'll find out how normal it really is.

On the flip side, consider today's corporate executives. They are young and old, black and white, rich and richer. These are the executives that take their perks and then cry that their organizations need to cut pension contributions. Former American Airlines CEO Don Carty got in deep trouble for allegedly hiding executive bonuses, even as the airline was on the verge of collapse. I wonder what the rank and file thought of their top leader's actions. Would those employees be engaged and dedicated? Remember, if it's all about me, then it can never be about you. That should be the slogan for many of these selfish leaders.

GOOD TIMING

As it has been said before, timing is everything. What really matters is how good the timing is. In other words, you need to know when to accelerate and when to put on the brakes. Like the racecar driver, you must accelerate in the straightaways and brake a little in the turns. For example, if you have an opportunity in your job to do more of what you're great at, then accelerate. If your work causes you so much stress that you can't sleep at night, then brake. If you get this, you'll have good results with your journey through success. Notice the reference to journey, because that's exactly what it is. We never arrive!

In my journey, this was the toughest lesson to learn. Maybe like you, I kept my focus on an outcome I thought would deliver satisfaction. The misaligned voices in my head said, "When I make this level of income, then I'm going to slow down" and "I'm doing this for my kids." Perhaps you've heard these voices, too.

Unfortunately, when you are in a race for success, you miss things along the way that are central in your development, like the concept that success was meant to chase you, not the other way around. The key is remembering that success is a result of the process; the process is where all the "gold" is mined.

LETTING GO

In order to give up the chase of success, you must let go. That's right, take your hands off the wheel and let go of everything you think you have control over. What is it in your life you can't stop obsessing about? What causes you to be there physically, but to be absent mentally? When you can't stop, there is a problem. Can you let go? If the thought makes you nervous, then you've built a habit.

It will be challenging to turn around (I hope you desire challenge by now), but your life is depending on you. Transformation and determination do not develop overnight. I don't care if you're the CEO of a Fortune 500 company.

Try taking the risk of living by your priorities for the next seven days. Take your life priorities and rank them. Next, be a slave to them. Yes, you're the slave, and your priorities are the master. If your relationship with family is number one, then let that dictate your schedule for the period of seven days. You won't get fired, but your family might look at you strangely. At the end of the seven days, ask your family if they felt like they were number one.

How are your emotional muscles feeling now that you've started to exercise again? The results of this test might astound you. You probably feel more balance and more alignment, don't you? If you're not careful, you might make these changes permanent. This would bode well for a world in need of more daring, and caring, people.

Now think about the things you equate with success. For example, maybe you're a talented musician. As a musician, you have received confirmation that you're skilled enough to perform in front of an audience. In addition, the idea of playing gives you great pleasure. It almost produces a longing to play all the time. Here's the point, do you really think you need to obsess, stress, or fret over the success of playing live? No, because it's your destiny and you were hardwired to play music. The fabric of your life is woven with this reality.

Notice I didn't once mention you shouldn't work on getting better at whatever you're hardwired to do. Some might mistake my insights as a free ticket or a sit-back-and-do-nothing approach. Nothing could be further from the truth. Working on getting better is the process. Success is what comes from the work/process. Be careful not to miss the connection.

REDEFINING

Redefining what success means is a great companion to the first lesson of living by your priorities. Think of it this way, what if you had all the money and time you needed? How would you define success in light of that reality? Money and things wouldn't make the list because you've already got them. Time wouldn't be an issue either, so what's left? My guess is you'd be free to look into the things that make you smile. Would you volunteer at that battered women's shelter? Would you serve on a community board? Success should be a matter of the heart with the mind managing the progress.

Scary indeed is the journey to discovery. Most people pay so little attention to the things they truly long for they are astounded by what lies within them. If you're not careful, you'll try to talk yourself out of pursuing your true desires. You might even try to run back to "Egypt."

My good friend Linda Larger said making changes in your life is like those stress balls. You squeeze tightly and the ball goes the way you desire. When you loosen the pressure, the ball returns to the shape it was before you squeezed it. As Linda would describe, when we feel pressed, we make changes to adjust to the pressure. When things get "better," we go back to old habits. The trick is to make a daily decision to support the changes you've made. Anything less than that will more than likely lead to disappointment.

So you see, redefining success is key but risky. The path of wealth without meaning is a lonely place. I spent many years trying to use wealth and material success to prop up my self-worth.

Sadly, most of your universe won't even question your motives let alone whether you're chasing success. That's why advisors who could care less about your net worth are essential. They will make you uncomfortable, and they will make you accountable. We need accountability!

We need peace inside our successes. Your worth is so much more than a dollar. Are you willing to experience the short-term pain of redefining success?

BIG-PICTURE PERSPECTIVE

Author and thought leader J. Robert Clinton has said that leaders who finish well have the knack for big-picture thinking. Big-picture thinking is more than a talking point in a senior management meeting. In this arena, it is the ability to see the horizon of your lifetime—that's right, from birth to death. You need to ask yourself, "Where have I been?" "Where am I going?" and, of course, "Where am I now?" The birth idea is easy to absorb, but the death part is another matter. As much as we try to avoid the subject of death, it's important in order to gain perspective. That perspective will help as you seek to stop the chase of success.

Not long ago, a family friend, Sandra, died of cancer. Needless to say, it was a painful experience. Eileen and I had lost touch with this woman, but we always remained close to her in heart. She was only thirty-nine years old and left behind a husband and two young children. Eileen was a bridesmaid at her wedding. It doesn't seem real for her to be gone. Memories can fool us into believing things happened yesterday. You forget that time goes by so quickly.

A month or so after the funeral, I had the opportunity to have lunch with Sandra's husband, Rick. It struck me how composed he seemed, especially considering the devastation he was working through. As you can imagine, raising two kids alone is a daunting prospect. Sandra was such an integral part of their lives. Parenting is tough for two people, let alone just one. As I looked into Rick's eyes, I knew I was a spectator...someone who had never experienced his level of pain.

One area that reminded me composure only goes so far was the issue of the holidays. Rick knew the holiday season would be especially tough. Sandra was at her best during Christmas. Eileen once told me Sandra would play holiday music all year long. I didn't realize until she was gone what a special, mystical time the holidays were for Sandra and Rick.

As Rick and I slowly ordered our lunches, the conversation turned to happiness. His comments were inspiring, but one stood out from all the rest. He told me he had been blessed to have fourteen years with his beloved wife, and some never get that long. He was thankful inside the lifetime he'd been given.

I froze, knowing that a life without Eileen would be unimaginable. Wow! How would I live? How would I take care of our two children? The drive back to my office was filled with amazement and introspection. How powerful Rick's words were. This experience helped me see that life is a broad spectrum full of twists and turns. Regardless of which ones we face, the lesson remains the same. We must deal with each issue and manage it over a lifetime. Rick gave me a lesson in big-picture thinking that will stay with me for the rest of my days.

A lifetime perspective is the essence of big-picture thinking. If you adopt this perspective, you will learn to chase the things that matter. A great example would be your daughter's dance recital or your son's spelling bee. If you're like many Americans, the chasing of success has left you out of breath. You're bone tired and looking for a break. Big-picture thinking introduces you to the world of satisfaction and contentment. It will help you breathe.

Remember the great marathon runner Roger Bannister. He recognized that sprinting was not his greatest asset. His greatest asset was his pace. What if you took that approach with your life? What if you paced yourself so success in life came ahead of success in work?

We need to look over the horizon and see things from the beginning to the finish line. It means pacing ourselves for the long run, the marathon of life. Success wants to follow. It wants to provide you with the water as you hit your stride. It wants you to give up the career and find a magnificent life. The question remains, will you listen to success?

SECRET 4
Beware of the Evil Number Seventeen

*"Do not seek to follow in the footsteps of
the wise. Seek what they sought."*

--Matsuo Basho

Okay, I know the title of this chapter is a little strange, but don't go anywhere. The Evil Number Seventeen is more normal than you might think. Why? It's because a number of people allow the seventeenth thing on their list to become number one on their list. We'll explore why and how to reorder our lives later, but right now, let's explore the origin of this dreaded way of life.

PLANNING

Some years ago two companies were at the forefront of planning. Franklin Planner and Daytimer became the norm for time management. I'm sure there were others, but those two were the most popular during the mid- to late eighties. They produced tools to help busy workers/executives stay on top of their days, or schedules for that matter. Henry Ford would have been proud.

It made total sense to adopt the principals of these planning tools. Who would want to be inefficient at work and life? The intentions of both plans were noble. Get people more organized and you'd get more productivity.

The problem with these systems was two-fold. One, human beings are human beings. Two, there wasn't enough emphasis on what was most important. (That changed with Franklin when they merged with Stephen Covey's organization.)

Human beings in the last few decades were not known for their self-discipline. Therefore, time management became like diets. People were always searching for the next thing to help them manage time better. The lack of self-discipline also contributed to a lack of prioritization in life and work. We became wanderers.

Today we have smartphones, electronic calendars, PDAs, and the list goes on. Are we any more efficient or productive? Maybe we are in some ways, but in many important ways, we're not. For example, take Jason. I've known him for over ten years. He's been to all the classes, has the book on tape, and appears to be together. But he still hasn't taken the time to figure out why he should bother with things he's involved in, such as the five daily meetings that go on for longer than they should.

For all the talk about technology and its transforming power, people still lack vision, and they, in turn, don't have clear direction. This plague is constantly showing up in Corporate America. We learned how to make money, but we can't answer the question of why we did it.

This is where the Evil Number Seventeen comes in to wreck our best-laid plans. We make our to-do list, which is invariably too long, and we set off to conquer the day. Unfortunately, and I'm not sure how or why, number seventeen screams at us for attention. You'd think there was a conspiracy afoot. In a world of loudness we pay attention to what screams the loudest.

Why do we feel the loudest thing is the most important? More often than not, it's because we're not sure if our deepest and most prized priorities are still awake. We confuse decibels with substance.

The most important things in life don't scream for attention (at least until we're close to disaster). They figure you know to pay attention to them. You may wonder what happens if we ignore our highest priorities for too long. More often than not, you'll become like the boxer who, after winning many bouts, believes he doesn't need to train with dedication because of past successes. Like the boxer, if you fail to train, you may find yourself knocked out.

PRIORITIES MATTER

You have an opportunity now to impact what the future will be. You must start today by discovering and owning your priorities. For the sake of your interest and page pace, I'll assume you know what priorities are—the things most important to you. Failure to think about these things will keep you chasing your tail.

Tracy was a person who failed to own her priorities. She always had the best of intentions, and she was always tired—just like the dog that chases its tail. When we met, Tracy's priority issues were not apparent to me. But after conducting a workshop, where she was a participant, it became clear. She was beginning to experience the atrophy that comes from neglecting priorities. Tracy could quote the corporate motto many times over. However, she didn't realize the organization she worked for was also waning from years of neglecting its priorities. Therefore, all the wonderful performance reviews could not save her.

The workshop I gave happened to be on the Evil Number Seventeen. Tracy looked at me with great sincerity during the presentation. She reminded me of someone who really wanted a better way of working and living. I encouraged her, as well as the other participants, to start building new habits—the type of habits that encourage personal and professional growth. You may be familiar with the principle that a habit can be formed in twenty-one days.

Sadly, I don't know if Tracy ever made it to the other side of owning her time and priorities. But one thing is for sure; she represents the plight of many. These are the men and women who have no long-term strategies—personal or professional. Sadly, these same people work for entities that never seem to get around to investing in their employees and, therefore, set poor examples of establishing and acting on priorities. These organizations are aiding and abetting the Evil Number Seventeen. And believe me, the Evil Number Seventeen does not rest. He will continue to bug you until you make a habit of submitting to your priorities.

A BETTER PLACE

What if we all had only five priorities and we focused on those alone? What would your world look like? Could you catch your breath in that place? My guess is the answers to those questions make you smile and maybe feel a little sad. You will smile because you want that reality. You're sad because it seems impossible. Take heart as we begin to discover how things should be. I see a better place, where your best intentions are no longer just intentions, but living reality.

Scott is someone I've known for many years who lives that type of reality. In many ways, he's an inspiration and a real example of focus and brilliance. He told me about a time when he was called on to speak about his area of responsibility with a large regional bank. It was a divisional type of meeting with many upper-level managers in attendance. Oddly (or not), Scott was asked to speak from a script given to him by his boss—talking points for the "working dead" you might call it. The only problem was that Scott was not a part of the "working dead."

Scott was a "tell-it-like-it-is" leader. He believed the heart of the leader should drive the content of any speech or conversation. Scott went in cold. Keep in mind he knew what was most important. And that was what his audience got. The Evil Number Seventeen had no place in Scott's agenda. He knew what was important that day. He lived it out with utter ease. (You can do that when you know what's most important.) Ironically, many of his co-workers wondered where he got his talking points. They were shocked when he told them the points came from his heart.

There are only about five things in life and work that are truly important. (You have to decide what they are…choose carefully.) Find those five things, and don't keep adding to the list. You need to stay focused. You can't be focused with a list of ten or fifteen items. I don't care what our culture says about "having it all." You can't have it all, and you don't want it all even if you could. Look back over your life and examine what has stood the test of time. Was it the books you read or the important relationships with other people? The answer to that question will reveal a lot about what should be most important to you.

BALL OF CONFUSION

Since the advent of the information age, we've been inundated with more than we can digest. They come from television, the Internet, radio, and print media—thousands of messages with an ever-faster de-livery. Every part of life seems to have accelerated to match this mad-dening pace.

What do we do to keep our sanity on this ball of confusion? Start doing nothing. That's right; start doing nothing. Take a step away and reorder everything. Watch how the world just keeps on turning. The world system doesn't care about you...never has, never will. Are you shocked? Okay, take this test: Does the rest of the world slow down when you do? No, it just asks you to get back on the treadmill.

Jeff came to me by chance and asked me to give him a little advice on career planning. His situation was not unlike many. Jeff wasn't clear about where he should start, so I recommended he start by identifying things that make him come alive. At that point, Jeff and I went through the process of discovery. This included casting a vision around the discovery, the needed growth planning for the vision, and how to live out the process on a daily basis.

The habit we discussed first was choices around how we spend our time. More than likely, Jeff was like most men. After work, he would sit down in front of the television and veg. I never directly asked him how much time he spent on veg activity, but it was a safe assumption it could last for hours. The assumption was safe because I asked him if he watched the television program *American Idol*. With a nod, he gave me all the response I needed. I immediately asked him when *American Idol* last helped him with his destiny. Further, I asked when this program last helped him catch his dreams. With a look of someone making a connection, Jeff made it clear the answer was never.

Jeff didn't need to give up television (though that would not be the worst thing for any of us); he just needed to put the first things first. There will always be some type of "American Idol," but there won't always be a life to live.

I'VE GOT TIME

You would think that America is a nation of people under age twenty-five. Our wasting of time is evidence of this. Author Max Lucado once wrote that modern man believes he is forever young, and eternity is a lifetime away. This idea is so appropriate for the world in which we live today. We have a mindset that we can get to it later. Does anyone know when his or her last breath will be? No! Then how does anyone know they will have a "later"?

Think of the baby boomers today. They made an endless pursuit of leaving marks in the sand, only to have them swept away by a tide of futility. There are even those in the boomer generation who believe we'll eventually live forever. Their faith in science and technology is astounding.

Fortune featured an article some time ago about genetics and slowing (if not eliminating) the aging process. The premise was rooted in genetic therapy. For example, as certain organs, cells, etc., deteriorate, new ones can be regenerated. By doing this, you have instant Ponce De Leon and his fountain of youth.

I'm all for science and technology improving life. I have Type I diabetes, and the insulin pump I use has dramatically improved my health. To say my lifestyle has changed for the better would be an understatement. But the truth rules here: nobody gets out of this life alive.

THE LAZY RIVER

Are you comfortable considering laziness? I hope you are, because I'm going there. Laziness in the physical sense is bad, but mental and emotional laziness is downright suicide. As America continues to advance in areas like science and technology, the recipients get lazier. We'll spend hours each week watching *Desperate Housewives* and shows like it, but we won't spend ten minutes reading a book on growth.

Do those who consume mass amounts of television suffer from boredom? Yes they do, and that sets the stage for laziness. Do you see the danger? When laziness creates the vegetative state, you will find it hard to know what's most important. You will also lack the will to do anything about it. Americans need to get back to practicing—practicing like an athlete preparing for an important competition.

THE POWER OF THE WILL

Arnold Palmer once said winning wasn't everything, but the will to win was. How right he was and is. However, it appears our culture today wants the slam-dunk and nothing less. The idea that some things are just gutted out is way out of the norm.

Learning to settle for less than a shutout is harder when many are seemingly very successful without much effort. Ladies and gentlemen, these "successful" people are the few cursed souls. "Cursed?" you may ask. Absolutely. Anything that comes easy is poisonous to mind, body, and soul. Please remember, with information so readily available, you will get to see more stories about the "few." We're living in the land of information overload. Besides, any network executive will tell you, it's much more glamorous to look at the person who's seemingly got it all.

The question still remains as to our will to win. There's power in the idea of winning in our pursuit of the right priorities and directions. Don't be fooled by the messages of leisure and get-it-fast avenues. They're from the P.T. Barnum school of priorities. Having the will to do it right comes from a desire to meet and become one with destiny.

You have a purpose worth pursuing. You may not hit it every time, but it is your lifelong aim. Stand or fall, you won't give up. This describes the power of the will.

My friend Beth is a wonderful example of the power of will. When we first met, she could be best described as a skeptic. She didn't buy into much of anything I said or did. It must be noted that those she was exposed to previously were not examples of good influence. Their perspective was more rooted in getting the job done. These types of leaders tend to see people as a means to an end and nothing more.

Fortunately, Beth and I eventually connected, and all I had to do was get out of her way. She took to her growth and destiny like bird to sky. She started asking herself what was important. Beth wanted a life of meaning and success. She had her setbacks (letters that indicated someone else was picked for the job opportunity), but she kept going. Whether it was a class or a networking opportunity, Beth never let her setbacks paralyze and thwart her dreams. She kept moving forward despite those frustrating obstacles.

At the time of this writing, Beth is going through what author and leadership coach Terry Walling calls "transition." Transitions can be a place of pain and a place of preparation. Transitions are where the will is tested. Robin may not fully grasp it right now, but she is more successful than she knows. She has her priorities aligned with her vision of the future, and turning back is not an option. Pity the poor souls who don't even consider exploring their destinies and adopting the will to pursue them.

THINKING DIFFERENTLY

Somewhere in my past, a wise sage told me if I wanted to change my behavior, I needed to change my thinking. This is the place where you can put old Evil Number Seventeen to rest—permanently. You will face challenges in doing this, but you will be rewarded. It will feel awkward, but you'll get used to it. So take heart; the journey is worth the pain. I speak from experience but, more importantly, from liberation.

Consider for a moment the established patterns you have in thinking. For example, what's your routine in the morning? My guess is you have a specific pattern you stick to. You are human, so the comfort you feel in following your pattern is not so strange.

Now think for a moment. (Yes, I know, this is the section on thinking.) Just imagine you have to do everything differently than you're used to. What once was left is now right. What once was the freeway is now urban streets. That scares you a little, doesn't it? It would not only feel weird but downright awkward. You might be surprised at how you would adapt if you made a decision to make things work for the better.

Fear not, this is not an exercise in motivational fear. I just want to alert you to the upfront pain that comes with battling Mr. Seventeen. Just think for a moment how it would be.

POURING THE CEMENT

The only way you can start to cement some change in your time and priorities is to decide. That's right; you need to make a specific decision to own your change. Owning means making a decision to possess. So what do you own; and, more importantly, what is most important to you?

When I was ready to pour the cement in my life, I set my priorities based on my heart. From most to least important, they ranked: God, family, health, extended family/friends, and work. I imagined how it would be to stand in front of God and show Him this list. The scary part after writing the list was wondering if I could really keep things in the proper order. It was tough! But I decided that being a success in life meant staying true to my priorities. I know I got the order right because that ranking still stands today.

One area that dogged me for years was how far down work was on my list. In the American culture, work is the veritable holy grail. We don't talk about it because, deep down, we're ashamed. We know a successful life is more important, but we lack courage to embrace it. Sometimes this happens due to greed or some deep-seated insecurity. Both of these are equally harming to you as you set your sights on shedding the control work has in your life. In some ways, this puts into perspective why some people will literally kill themselves through work.

Here's a little anecdote I used when I worked in Corporate America. I asked myself where I ranked in the corporation's priorities. Yes, corporations have priorities, whether they acknowledge them or not. It struck me that I was as far down on their list as they were on mine. Wake up call! That confirmed to me that work was ranked where it was supposed to be.

Ironically, work always moved up my priority list when my insecurities got the better of me. You know what I mean—the need to be liked, the fear of rejection, and so many more. Love your work, not your employer, because employers find it difficult to love back.

THE HOW-TO

If something is important you'll write it down. This is the second step after making the decision to change your time and priorities. After the writing, you need to keep the content with you wherever you go. Keep it on your notebook computer, your PDA, a laminated piece of paper—you get the point. Why do this? You're human, which means you have a tendency to forget about what's not in front of you. Remember the thousands (if not millions) of messages coming at you every day? It's important to be intentional about keeping your priority message in front of all the others.

Tom was a part of a work group I led some years ago. He hungered to line up his passions with his vocation. It was rare and beautiful to witness. Here this guy was working in a mediocre company, yet he could see past all the fog. He caught fire where fires rarely happened. Certainly, there was something inside Tom that craved something better.

In one workshop/growth session, Tom realized he wasn't being true to his priorities in the work he was doing. We had a section of the workshop dedicated to partnering with another member of the work group. Tom and his partner had a joint light go off. Tom wanted to be involved with numbers rather than customer relations—the job he was doing. He had the career background for numbers and loved working in that environment, so his journey to right things began. He didn't panic; he planned. This is important to note because many do panic. We tend to believe the end is always near.

Why was Tom successful in finding a position working with numbers? He knew what his priorities were, he had them written down, and he stood by them. It is very important to remember that words, phrases, and meaning are powerful motivators. They are keys to a successful life. Tom realized this and stayed committed to that end. Was it a painless experience? Of course not; nothing of great value comes without a great price.

ARE YOU DOING WHAT YOU SAY?

The last component of getting things going is accountability. Who and what are holding you accountable to those priorities of yours? Is it your spouse? Is it your rabbi? If the answer is no one, then you're doomed. Sorry for such a strong statement, but I've seen many men and women start strong only to fizzle out. More times than not, it was because they had no one around them to ask questions of accountability.

It's easy for people to grow indifferent to guidance and transparency. We'd rather keep secrets. We think there's always a place to hide. We forget that eventually secrets can and do come to light.

Human nature craves comfort, order, and predictability. Why do you think people lose it when road construction occurs in their neck of the woods? We want things to go the way we want them to, when we want them to. The road to getting the Evil Number Seventeen out of the picture is in direct contradiction to those human cravings. It can be painful to ignore something that has been bugging us for a lifetime. More than likely, you'll give up on changing and right-sizing your priorities without accountability.

The following are some people who've held me accountable over my lifetime:

+ My beloved wife, Eileen

+ My dear friends Harvey Hook, Rick Williams, and Larcel McGhee

+ Colleagues like J.A Dava and Jeff Hayes

+ Great writers and teachers

+ My Lord and Savior, Jesus Christ

Your list doesn't have to look just like mine, but I think you get the point. The journey is long, and it can't be successfully run alone. So who's running beside you?

SECRET 5
Watercooler Conversations

Every spoken word is either rain or sun to the hearer.

--Author Unknown

Think of all the conversations you've ever had. That would make for a long list if you've lived any amount of time. If you're like me, you won't remember them all, but some conversations stick with you. The ones that seem to last forever are the focus of this chapter. If nothing else, you might get a better understanding of the power behind words. Maybe you'll gain an appreciation for listening, which is a great tool for communication. Part of my waking up came through overhearing and participating in these watercooler conversations.

The following interactions were taken from conversations I've been in directly or ones that were relayed to me directly. They're honest, poignant, and even funny. Some are snapshots and some are portraits, but every conversation at the watercooler reflects a story. Sometimes these stories are grand, and sometimes they are small. Either way, they all communicate the state of people in Corporate America today. So put your ears in gear and listen…

A STORY OF TALENT

It was a hot summer morning in July. Angela caught me walking toward the stairs and asked me to stop. I obliged and an unexpected conversation began.

Angela was one of the most talented performers in the organization. You'd expect strong opinions and anecdotes from someone like her. Type A personality with a dash of deep thinking described her.

I'd known Angela for almost five years. We'd talked before, but most of those conversations would be classified as surface talk. I got the feeling this conversation would be different. Things were kept on the surface at first, but her eyes revealed more. I stayed as she began to go deeper.

It seemed she had just suffered through another meeting of corporate fluff—wasted time spent saying things not really meant. At first appearance, I thought she was truly bothered by the content of her meeting, but I tuned my hearing to a deeper frequency. This enabled me to understand where she was truly coming from.

You see, Angela was not that concerned about the meeting or its content. Angela was concerned about her life. That's right, her life. I would guess she was north of forty, but it was clear time mattered to her. Can you blame her? Who wants to waste away their life in an endeavor that more than likely will be forgotten in next quarter's earnings release? Human beings are funny that way; they see themselves as more valuable than the numbers.

It struck me that her tone began to rise in intensity as she relayed how long she had given herself to the organization. She was part of the working dead that was trying her best to wake up. Angela wanted me to affirm her and her feelings, which I did. I did this without many words because sometimes listening is the greatest form of communication we have.

She went on to say that she felt like her life was wasting away before her eyes. This was a life that once was sure of the path ahead—a life unwavering. I told her she could do something about it—a statement that reminded her of an often forgotten reality that we have a unique DNA for a reason. Find the reason, find meaning. Angela wanted this reality to be true. I wondered how badly she wanted that kind of life.

As the conversation lingered on, Angela began to tear up. I knew then there were issues running deeply in the place we call career. What a strange dichotomy—here we were by coincidence with her feeling trapped. Whether at her own doing, or by some subtle deception, Angela wondered if the life she dreamed of had passed her by. Sometimes this state creates panic or a feeling of surrender. Either way, the person is wrapped tightly in his or her chains.

AREN'T YOU AFRAID?

Margie was nervous. This was not so strange for someone who seemed that way a lot of the time. However, this time was more pronounced. Inside, I began to wonder if I should get nervous too, just to balance everything out. Of course, that would have only made things worse. "So, Margie, how are you?" I asked.

"Aren't you nervous?" she replied. It didn't take long to figure out that Margie got especially nervous about people with titles. She knew I was expected in a meeting with a senior-level manager to discuss a potential promotion.

Margie went on to tell me about her experience with this particular manager. It was clear the encounter had unnerved her. Was she intimidated or flat-out scared? Maybe she was looking for praise and honor but never received it. Either way, her face betrayed her words. Astounding! Margie managed a group of fifty plus people. Didn't she understand the dynamics of grace under pressure? It's doubtful she did because most organizations fail to teach their people such things. Margie never revealed what happened, but it was clear the experience had shaken her.

I wasn't nervous about my pending meeting and told her accordingly. In some ways, it was important for Margie to know how I felt. I was compelled to communicate that some things are out of our control. Who knew what would come of my chat with that manager? Frankly, I had no power over the outcome. Just the same, Margie looked at me with quizzical eyes and walked away thinking (I can only imagine) I was from Mars.

I thought about my brief encounter with Margie later. Was Margie usually composed and collected? No, she was impressed and enamored with personality. She wasn't affected so much by the executive as by the power behind the suit. Margie looked at an upper-level position in an organization and immediately attributed all things wonderful to the person. Evidently, no one ever told her that, as the great Peter Drucker once said, leadership implies responsibility, not privilege.

JUST OK

This conversation resonates with me still today, even though it happened several years ago. The work group I was leading at the time was just beginning to execute on the plan. We were given high goals of sales and profit. That reality was important because we were so close to moving from average to above-average.

Sheila and I spoke often. She was what I call a trusted advisor. We were talking about the performance of my work group and what was missing in their execution. An analytical personality (like mine) would question whether their deficits were the result of work pressures, outside influences, and the like. But she told me the answer was simple— the people were OK with being OK. I asked her to elaborate.

Sheila revealed to me that many people are content with average, especially if average is what they have been used to. When average delivers food, shelter, and money, why question the status quo? She pointed out that one certain associate had never, in all the years they had known each other, wanted anything more than average. Sheila looked at me and said, "If you're OK with being OK, then you have no motivation to change."

After pausing to reflect, I asked Sheila if she thought I was crazy for wanting to bring change to these people. She replied that it was impossible to change them. Her assessment brought a chill to my spine. Until that time, I thought I could persuade just about anyone to see things differently. Sheila reminded me that people must want change before they can accept it. That's the only type of change that will stick.

Though she didn't know it at the time, Sheila was describing the "working dead." These are people who allow the slumber of average to permeate everything.

The sobering reality set in that day. Would I take to heart Sheila's observation? Would this observation set my path toward one single-minded mission? The writing of this book is evidence enough.

EXCUSE #499

Jason was a reasonably patient man, but every person has a limit to how much patience he or she can muster. I was watching him closely hoping he would keep his cool. Why? Jason was about to hear the same excuse for the 499th time. Of course I may be wrong, maybe it was the 500th time. Anyway, can you imagine the level of frustration he must have felt?

The context for this related to one of Jason's peers who had responsibility for a product/service offered by the organization. This was a vital service for what Jason did. If it helps, Jason was in sales. Salespeople depend on inside support, so Jason had a vested interest in what his peer had to say. His paycheck was on the line, so you understand how red Jason's face would get.

In Jason's world, he competed with many types of entities. Some were small outfits that were nimble and quick, while others were large with massive resources. These realities didn't scare Jason. He had that rare confidence that kept him focused on winning. At the end of the day, Jason wanted to win. He would often ask me if I thought the organization really wanted to win.

As with many organizations, environments could get rough and complex. Whenever those environments got sticky and tough, Jason's peer would use the same excuse for why nothing could be done.

On this occasion, we had just made it through the first third of a meeting. It came time to begin the Q&A about the market. As expected, Jason's peer spoke what we had all heard before. This time, and in front of the company president, Jason was going to speak his mind. He seized the moment to comment, "Why is it that we must always sit by and watch what other competitors do before we act?" It was a classic rhetorical question.

The look of shock on his peer's face was priceless. The manager (Jason's peer) tried some variation on his statement but stumbled just the same. Unfazed by the discomfort in the air, Jason continued, "I've spent the last five years building a business around certain products and pricing, and when things get rough, you say we need to wait until the big boys get rationale. I can't keep changing the script to reflect our inability to keep up."

After many "ums" and "buts," it was clear that a white flag needed to go up. But white flags were rare in that atmosphere. Facing the ugly truth was the last thing we were going to get in that meeting. As you might have guessed, a suggestion of another meeting and research was made. Jason surprised me and decided to back off. I think he realized the cold reality of the situation: when people don't know something, they don't know what to do.

After the meeting, I took Jason aside and asked him how he was doing. He replied that he was fine. Jason's last comment is what I remember most. He said, "I just want them to fix the problem so we can move on with the plan as directed. It really is that simple, Eric."

When you're in a place where getting things done seems to be secondary, it can be easy to get frustrated. Jason was a doer, which made lame excuses even more of an issue for him.

WHY MANAGE PEOPLE?

This brief conversation came from the comment section of my blog on the Epic Living Web site. Jim is the writer and the person who experienced the event. I am amazed at the rare honesty he got from his boss. Usually there isn't this much transparency in Corporate America.

Jack relayed the following:

The other day, I asked my boss what was the most important thing that I did for him and he said, 'Manage the group the way I should have managed it.' Believe it or not, this individual is a senior leader. This encounter was not the first in what used to cease and amaze me. It allows me to add my 2 cents worth on your blog now and then. So as Eric puts so eloquently, be honest with yourself. Ask yourself do you respect your boss and what he/she stands for? Do you respect the company you work for? Do you like what it stands for? Do you like what it does? Does it care about you and its customers? Does it have a plan for the future, or is it living in the past? The fact is that not all companies are created equal. There are bad, good, and great companies, and they all treat their people in radically different ways.

When was the last time you decided to look beneath the surface of your organization? You might find some surprises like Jack.

WE'RE A CULT

You know you're in trouble when your organization wants to control speech and thoughts. This is the approach most cults use to keep followers in line. I've often wondered why some organizations feel this approach works. Most of the time, they've just flat-out run out of ideas. So when Randy sent this comment, his first on a blog I might add, it was a perfect snapshot for this chapter.

I can only comment on my many years of association with banks. I would have to say that the majority of banks that I communicate with operate more like cults than a thriving enterprise. As you stated, they are more interested in spending most of their time on what happens internally such as policies, procedures and meetings that are a complete waste of time. Unfortunately, that mindset only serves the needs of a few executives and the insightful, innovative employees make a quick exit. I cannot see how anyone can truly thrive in a cult corporation.

Does his comment ring true for you? Do you have a manager who wants you to think a certain way? Ask the person sitting three cubes over and I bet you'll find you're not crazy.

THE REASON I NAMED IT EPIC LIVING

A friend once asked me why I named my organization Epic Living. As he looked at me, I traveled back in time to a place not revisited often. It was a painful time and not a place of fondness for me. I relayed a story from my days as a senior manager for a financial services firm. This story goes back five years ago.

I was at the regular weekly staff meeting, and I was used to these meetings taking what seemed like forever. This meeting was one of those engagements where it took two hours to get to fifteen minutes worth of information. I was a good soldier, so consequently, I endured—endured countless points; counterpoints; and, last but not least, grandstanding.

At this particular meeting, we found ourselves drifting into a discussion about dress codes. Naively, I expected this discussion to last ten minutes, but we went for forty-five. What I found interesting was how easy it was to answer questions with just a word or two. Don't misunderstand; my answers were sincere. It just proved to me we didn't need to spend that much time on something so small.

Because I had already checked out, I pulled out my planner and began to jot down a few thoughts. As I felt the regret of seeing two hours of my life pass by, I wrote, "I must live an Epic Life." It stuck with me, and it spurred me on in ways I couldn't have known then. How would I live an Epic Life? What would it look like against the backdrop of my career? It was a defining moment that birthed the organization I founded.

Patrick Lancione wrote a book titled *Death by Meeting*. I've never read it, but the title is priceless. My experience inside most organizations is that meetings are time killers designed to give managers a sense of purpose. They usually run too long and don't produce meaningful execution. Next time you're in a meeting, time it, and at the end, evaluate what percent was really useful. If you justify these get-togethers, you may be asleep.

DON'T FORGET ABOUT ME!

When Christine sent me an e-mail about reminding her boss of her value, it kind of surprised me. I wasn't surprised because she hadn't made stands in the past, but because I was no longer in the organization. We had worked together for almost seven years. Her story gave me a perspective (from the outside) that I hadn't experienced before.

In some organizations, many of the decisions seem to be made in a vacuum. Such was the case regarding a decision about Christine's reporting structure. Her boss was giving serious consideration to moving Christine to a less strategic area for her expertise of training. However, Christine didn't see how this move would compliment or help the division. So that begged the question: would she speak up?

Here is Christine's e-mail:

Hi Eric.

I accomplished something really important I wanted to tell you about. The last time we talked I mentioned feeling like my reporting structure would be changed to Anna. After sitting with this for a moment, I realized it was not something that I wanted or believed to be in my best interest so I made an appointment to talk to Erin (her boss).

I sat down with her and made my points explaining why I wanted to keep reporting to her, including moving to Anna would be a step backward for me, I had too much to offer to be back on the "line," and I didn't think Anna could offer me anything as my manager.

I know that reporting to Anna would not be a hardship, and I know reporting to Erin does not necessarily mean getting the kind of leadership I need, but I do know that in that particular world and mindset, I needed to make a statement out loud - to the world and to myself.

Ultimately, the decision is not mine to make, but I did what I wanted to do.

I read this great quote today and wanted to pass it along:

"I don't want to get to the end of my life and find that I have just lived the length of it. I want to have lived the width of it as well."

-Christine

How many of you would have just accepted your boss's decision without saying a word? I don't write that to indict, but to encourage you to remember it is your life. Taking a risk from the gut, which is what Christine did, produces greatness and not regret.

WHAT PLANET ARE YOU FROM?

If you embrace greatness and growth, some might think you're strange. Maybe we've accepted mediocrity as the norm for fear of the price of greatness. But Mike's story illustrates a breakthrough moment.

Mike told me, "I was interviewing for a position within the organization that would locate me closer to home. When the hiring manager met with me, I was pretty excited about the potential opportunity. After getting through the initial review of my resume, she asked me about my thoughts on the organization and how I fit into the picture. I explained in detail my growth in the last three years and how I have become more aware of leadership. She perked up a little as I went on to say how important it was to lead with purpose.

"I gave her my definition of leadership and let her know it was important for me to share that with a prospective manager. Additionally, I shared my vision with her. At that point, she seemed a little lost for words, but the look in her eyes said, 'What planet are you from?' In the end, it was a good and bad thing. I think she was impressed but at the same time somewhat puzzled."

Mike had a breakthrough because he realized his investment in his growth was not wasted. He discovered the power behind vision and growth.

When I first met Mike, he had the work ethic but seemed to be searching. Like most people I've led, he wanted something more than just doing a job. When I fast-forward to the present, I think Mike likes what he's found in himself. The rewards (promotions, money, etc.) have come as a result.

QUIET DESPERATION

Sometimes life does imitate art. This conversation occurred almost four years ago and still gives me chills. It was and is a powerful lesson on what not to be. Corporate America sometimes gives us clues where we least expect them. I was close to forty and wondering how my story would play out in the second half. Somewhere along the way, I learned that nothing is as it seems.

Alan and I were not close friends, but we got along well just the same. We ran different channels of business with common products, but we had different customers to serve. Like many co-workers, we would occasionally throw out the obligatory, "We need to do lunch sometime." Often, the lunch never happened, but in this case it did. The date was set, and I prepared myself for a normal lunch.

Alan and I met at a restaurant close to the office. As we sat down, the basics of business were addressed. He asked about my business, and I returned the favor. What came next caught me by surprise. The conversation turned toward the dreaded buyout scenario. Buyouts and mergers were very common in our industry. You just lived with it and got on with the tasks at hand. In this case, Alan lingered. He seemed genuinely concerned about the possibility of the organization being bought.

It dawned on me as we talked that I was having lunch with a man who was not in his thirties. Retirement was on his mind, as I clearly understood. He asked me my thoughts, but before I could answer, he began speculating about how long he could hang on. I'll never forget him saying, "If I can just make it five more years."

I sat there stunned and chilled. Questions raced through my head. Was this the common fate of all who climbed the corporate ladder? Would this be me in twenty years? Would I find myself just hanging on in quiet desperation, waiting for a retirement package? After a few minutes, Alan put his mask back on and the conversation went back to the obligatory. I think his last words were about needing to do lunch more often. Ironically or not, we never did have lunch again.

Well there you have it—conversations that happened via e-mail, one-on-one interaction, or group meeting. These conversations moved and changed me. Each one provided me with great inspiration to do more to help people grow. Most importantly, the conversations helped me understand that many people want to wake up in Corporate America.

SECRET 6
Embrace Reality

*"Don't stand in a bucket trying to lift
yourself up by the handle."*

--Winston Churchill

Let's get one thing straight; reality is the foundation of all great dreams. Many years ago, that statement would have made me uncomfortable. I was that dreamer type who believed anything was possible. I mean *anything* was possible. If you gave me a noble pursuit or a daring cause, I was ready to go.

I don't mean to burst your bubble, but some things should be left to theory and fantasy. Alas, some things are not meant to work out. As we move through this chapter, I'll explain how and why realistic thinking can be a tool to help our growth. Specifically, we'll examine you and how embracing reality can boost your growth—inside of work and out. Many of the following concepts may relate to your personal side, but remember, they still hold great relevance in your career.

IT BEGINS WITH A VISION

Visioning (as I call it), also known as dreaming, is a lost art. It has been relegated to the weird or to the famous. Those two groups are easily accepted as standard bearers for dreaming. One group we admire (the famous), and one group we shun (the weird). Realistic thinkers, on the other hand, are the ones who've supposedly settled down and have their heads on straight. They are the people who are focused on attacking the world as it is, not as they want it to be. They may be goal oriented, they may be practical, and they may even be a part of the working dead. At any rate, we appreciate them because of their predictability and dependability.

Realistic thinkers who are dynamic are the best type of visionaries. They believe success is a future-forward endeavor. They also see a better future than the current situation may indicate. Realistic thinkers know reality is a good barometer for the vision's timeline. They don't believe that just because they thought of something it means "go to market." For example, you believe your new product to improve workplace safety rings true in your head. Therefore, you're excited about the possibilities of a breakthrough, but you haven't consulted a soul on the viability. If you're a realistic thinker, you'll be willing to test the idea by thoroughly conferring with experts and advisors. Realistic thinkers are keen on assessing how their vision fits in today's world while seeing the future unseen. Realistic thinkers understand that the better future might be years away.

Many moons ago, a good friend gave me some striking information about a storm brewing within America's workplace. Fred was very knowledgeable in the area of human capital development. He spent many years impacting that reality within a Fortune 500 company. He said that in or around the year 2010, Corporate America will be in the midst of a worker shortage—a type of shortage not faced before. Key leadership positions as well as frontline knowledge workers will be impacted. Many experts believe there could be a gap of almost ten million more jobs than there will be people to fill them.

As I've alluded to in previous chapters, this is a reality that Corporate America and those working there have been slow to address. Lack of preparation for the coming worker shortage stems from the nasty habit of denial. Corporate America is too fixated on quarterly profits to address something so far into the future.

As I began to cast a vision around what I could see, I asked myself, how could organizations prepare and capitalize on this opportunity/problem? What would it mean for leaders in the area of growth development?

Asking questions was my next frontier. I asked people in the fields of human capital development, sales and marketing, and many others. I was astounded by the mix of opinions. Some believed people would just work longer; others thought Corporate America would eventually figure it out. I felt like the man who was trying to warn a building full of people about a bomb going off. All the while, I was failing to get them to realize the impending danger. Saying I was passionate about this subject would be an understatement.

Now here's the trick, are organizations today ready to follow your plan to start preparing for something that is three to five years away? Realistic thinking says, "Not yet." So how do you deal with the not yet? Frankly, you store your plan and never forget about it. By keeping your eyes on the world around you, you will eventually see when the time is right to capitalize. The key is not giving up and not allowing the vision to consume you.

Did I like hearing the voices in my head that kept saying those two words: not yet? Absolutely not, and I even tried to fight those voices—a struggle in vain that led me to a place I wasn't expecting. It was like arriving home for the first time. Reality was trying to help me. It didn't mean there wouldn't be an opportunity, it just meant not yet. Thank you, realistic thinking! If you don't allow realistic thinking to ground you, you could end up launching before the time is right.

HAVE IT REALITY'S WAY

We would rather not let reality get in the way of our own agendas. Our agendas become sacred cows demanding allegiance. Basically, we want things to go as we think or feel. In the end, though, reality has the final say. All our longings ultimately give in, and life is rendered as it truly is. Does this fact unnerve you? If it does, you're not alone. I struggled in this area longer than I care to admit. Regardless of the pain, the best outcomes come from our willingness to start on the ground. In other words, every flight must start on the runway.

In an organization I worked for many years ago, we exemplified vision held in balance by reality. Our performance fit the definition of how organizations and people can excel in the embrace of reality. The people were terrific (even when we disagreed). The commitment was real, and something wonderful was created. It was a time of tremendous growth and learning.

The group started as a mishmash of motivated and unmotivated people. As with many areas of life, the group's end was reflective of what was a wonderful ride. We had consecutive years of major growth and all seemed well. Although I was pleased with our success, as the leader of the group, it was my responsibility to keep an eye on the future. At that time, the future was revealing an end to the group as we had known it.

As I do in virtually every area of life, I consulted my advisors. I asked them if I was crazy. Was I being premature, or could things be moving in a different direction? Most of them agreed that things were on the move—toward a dismantling. New management was arriving (weekly it seemed), and it was clear they preferred a different approach.

Because many people had come to count on me for communicating clearly, I began to prepare the group for what I thought was ahead. It was not easy telling people to watch for a storm when there wasn't a cloud in the sky. When you're involved in something great, change of any kind is not a welcomed friend.

There was resistance to my views, but I pressed on because I knew preparation was essential. Tom Landry was a great head football coach of the Dallas Cowboys. He once said the role of a coach was to get men to do things they didn't want to do, so they could become all they've ever wanted to be. You should never hold back from a discovery you know in your gut is true. I didn't do this to the detriment of the organization. Moaning and complaining about the current state was not my style. What was essential was holding the need for clear communication and performance in tight tension. Everything was about continuing to give the organization growth, while advancing a realistic view of the future.

As the inevitable approached, I continued to speak with clarity and realism. And as those in the group found out, managing change can be better digested when the leader speaks from a standpoint of realistic thinking. In many ways, my unwavering focus on preparing for the reality to come made the change more palatable when it came. The leader must connect the dots before the followers do.

WHO DO YOU TRUST?

Leading yourself and others requires not only realistic thinking but also the art of building trust. Trust is vital in asking others to move to a different place. (You can put yourself in this category as well.) Trust provides people with the type of security that allows them to say, "I will go because I know you're committed to doing the right thing."

Leaders who are committed to doing the right thing are also committed to embracing reality. You'll never inspire people to something great if you can't help them understand how this principle applies. Besides, most organizations are too preoccupied with profits and ego to give their people realism. You can be a force for change.

THE KITE

Have you ever watched a kite flying in the middle of March? It conjures memories of childhood, doesn't it? As wonderful as this sight can be, it also can be an object lesson in why we can find ourselves ignoring reality. That kite is only as good as the holder of the string. If the person holding the string lets go or forgets to pay attention, there can be consequences. The kite could drift away in the blue sky above, or there might be a tangled mess in a tree.

In life, reality is designed to be the string that keeps a limit on wonderful flight. Without it, we would be wanderers floating without direction or, worse, tangled in a mess. We are sort of alive like the dancing kite, yet we're not fully there because we're tethered by the string of reality. This causes sadness and a feeling of helplessness. Therefore, we ignore the string—the reality—because we prefer to believe we have the freedom to fly without limits.

There are a number of executives and non-executives alike who ignore reality daily. They foolishly place too much confidence in their knowledge. Whether they hold tight to their advanced degrees or some other validation of their brainpower, they may be traveling on a disastrous road. The newspapers are filled with high-profile stories about smart people doing dumb things.

Where do we turn when we can't ignore reality? Do we proudly dig in our heels, as if to say, "I know what I'm doing?" Do we become fatalistic and convince ourselves that it really doesn't matter?

These responses occur in phases—life phases. In youth, pride can get a grip. There is a certain arrogance that screams invincibility. In many cases, this type of attitude closes off the opportunity to learn. In our youth, we can fall into the trap of thinking that learning is only useful when it serves our own purposes. Humility is the fertile ground needed for learning to occur.

Interestingly, by the time we reach middle age, fatalism can set in. We know taking bold stances won't make things any better. We know we're not young anymore, and life does have an end. We long for more but are not sure how to get it. This time is often called the midlife crisis. Bob Buford, the author of *Half Time,* says people must manage their midlife crises. Notice the implication of the inevitability of this season.

Even with all the forces of aging pressing against us, there's no guarantee humility will settle in and allow us to embrace reality. Often, a deadly dose of cynicism rears its head. One type of cynicism is a place where the person sees things in shades of black and more black. We find ourselves believing life is either worthless or meant to be used up in selfish pursuits. It really equates to giving up even when we pretend all is well. Conversely, if we allow reality to have its say, we might find a new and better way of operating. Cynicism never has and never will produce happy endings.

WHO'S TO BLAME?

Who do we point the finger at? Who's responsible for our lack of reality embrace? Certainly, Madison Avenue has some responsibility to bear, but let's face it, advertisers don't hold guns to our heads. The early influencers (parents, teachers, peers, etc.) come to mind, but again, we find ourselves not forced to follow. All in all, we are the ones to blame. Out there trying to fill the vacuum, we create our fantasies and run. We're running away from our fears or toward something we think will complete us. All the while, we leave reality in the dust.

Reality is often mistaken for an enemy. Usually this happens when things don't go the way we think they should. Michael was a Generation Y guy who personified this. He was a business analyst within a work group I led. Michael believed that as he dreamed it, so it would happen. What he forgot was that the stars were not hung in the sky just for him.

Dreams were everything to Michael, and his identity was connected to them as well. As Michael made his way through his twenties and into his thirties, he fell victim to the idea of eternal youth. He was running toward the fantasy that he would always be young and vigorous. Therefore, he missed many lessons along the way that would have helped him embrace the welcome realities of aging.

One contributor to Michael's roadblocks was the culture he operated in. America can be a place of illusions and seductions. So many things convince people they are exceptions to the laws that govern the universe. Michael gave in to these illusions. Whether this occurred consciously or unconsciously is a question mark. One thing is for sure; he missed a great opportunity to learn from those who had preceded him. I sometimes wonder if Michael ever learned the lesson about the value of realistic thinking.

NOBLE PURSUITS

What role should reality play when you believe you were destined to do something great? What if you've got the cure? What if God is on your side? I don't intend to offend anyone who has tied his or her pursuits to something noble. It's just that often we're not as noble as we claim, and that is evidenced by the absence of reality. We think our vision is unlimited. Of course this is not true, but we proceed on that basis. It just feels better to believe we were ordained for success. We'll look at emotions in the moment and drown in their pool.

I once was involved in leadership within a local church near my home in southeastern Ohio. One task we were tackling at that time was building a new church. After meeting in a school gymnasium for many years, we thought the time was right. Many of us wanted a true church building in which to worship. We were encouraged and maybe sold on the idea by an influential man in the congregation. He had a vision of the where, when, and how. Needless to say, he was very persuasive, especially with the senior pastor. He was also caught up in the euphoria of a new church. Maybe he thought a church building would validate the health of the institution.

As I listened to the plans, I got an ache in my stomach. This was my gut saying, "Not the right time, not the right leadership, and not the right people." But how could we turn away from something so right and noble? Sadly, I didn't speak up, and I got carried away as the others did. This was a lesson in listening to your gut. By throwing reality out the window, I allowed fantasy to take root. Your gut rarely steers you wrong.

Whether you ignore reality by intention or oversight, there are consequences when you fail to think realistically. Much misery came from that decision to build the church. A number of good friends were hurt; financial struggles ensued; and not too long after, I resigned my position and left the church altogether. Fortunately, the church survived this period and is thriving. I'm happy for those who are there now.

Breaks from reality bring lessons as well as consequences. In this case, a key lesson was the one around noble illusions. There are many noble pursuits—certainly not just building churches. An innovative technology or a new consumer product that would add quality to the lives of many would fit other definitions of noble. Regardless of the label, I learned that even the purest intentions are insufficient when glaring realities are ignored. Facing things as they are leads us to solid ground. Often, reality is trying to save you from disaster—if you're willing to listen.

INSIDE OUR FOUR WALLS

Maybe you've heard it said that organizations that are internally focused are destined for the trash heap. These organizations have a common dysfunction: they refuse to embrace reality. Focusing inwardly feels better and, therefore, provides insulation from realities of many colors. For example, the need for miracle numbers is a common delusion. The company spends many years believing long-term success in the marketplace would never change (and many senior managers perpetuated this belief). As time goes on, the organization stagnates.

Some years ago, I worked for an organization that had the same expectation. In a presentation, a senior leader told us flat out that we needed to make it happen or else. The graph he used reminded me of a rocket's trajectory—100 percent vertical. Insane? Yes, considering growth had never been that robust. The organization was desperate to save an enterprise close to implosion.

There are quite a number of reasons organizations (including their people) focus inwardly instead of outwardly. Maybe they have experienced too many wins. As contrary as that may sound, sometimes losing is as valuable as winning. Another common problem is leaders who've been in their positions too long. This happens when a board or other governing body is satisfied. I'm not recommending leaders be released for the sake of being released. We just need to evaluate performance on more than the numbers. Regardless of the reasons, internally focused organizations share the common trait of not embracing reality.

It has been said many enterprises are given early warnings about potential dangers. These warnings are usually given by people working inside. Some call them nuts or fear-mongers, but whatever you call them, they usually care a lot for the organization. Why else would these folks take on such risk? It's because they desire the best for all involved.

So why are they ignored? More than likely, it's because no one wants to believe something could derail the plans. Consider Winston Churchill in pre-World War II England or moderate Muslims who were predicting the rise of radical Islamic Jihadists. No one liked hearing what was rolling off their tongues.

Short-term priorities and expectations can cause panic among leaders—especially leaders who've never taken the time to look beyond the one-year plan. Their lack of humility makes it extremely difficult to get to meaningful solutions. Consequently, anyone who brings an unfriendly reality to the table is usually considered a threat. Threats need to be removed or conveniently ignored. Those in the mutual admiration society see the handling of threats as not only practical but also a needed move to protect the organization. They see themselves as working saviors but forget that reality is not created by a management team.

STORMS AHEAD

Reality will have the final say, and history will have another opportunity to weigh the choices in the balances. This was true for a fairly large financial services firm some years ago. Their problem was making bad loans to third parties—specifically, third parties that were not what you would call ethical. Not to mention, the company really didn't have a handle on who these customers were in the first place. The resulting losses reached such a level that the CEO decided to exit the business altogether. I was one of the original members of the division when the firm started making bad loans seven years before the collapse.

Interestingly, there were select people in that organization who repeatedly warned of trouble. As you can imagine, they were not listened to. Warnings about recklessness, inexperience, and general greed and folly were ignored. I can still remember certain managers who proclaimed that all was well. Everything was under control, they proudly announced.

What happened to those who dared to speak up? Initially, some were shunned and written off. (I always find it fascinating how some organizations can operate like cults.) Others persevered while attempting to be voices for quality and ethics. Eventually, the organization imploded and was acquired at a fraction of its original size. The new parent company kept some employees but downsized many others. It wasn't the type of ending you would have expected, considering how strong the organization was in the beginning.

SO WHAT DO I DO NOW?

Embracing reality comes down to a three-pronged approach. First, you must ask yourself if what you're doing is working or not working, and you must be honest about your answer to that question. Then you must have mentors/advisors who can give you perspective. Lastly, you must make a decision to accept reality—good or bad. This approach has served me well over the years. But know, sometimes embracing reality can be tough, if not downright painful. If you're willing to endure the short term, you'll be so far ahead in the game.

How often do you ask yourself whether what you're doing is working? Do you, like most people, wait until things are out of control before asking? I recommend you make a habit of asking this question come rain or shine. The answer will potentially be lifesaving to your endeavor, and at a minimum, it will provide an opportunity to correct or enhance.

During my days as a senior manager inside of Corporate America, I always gave talks on looking (consistently) at the progress being made in the first six months of selling. This time was crucial, and time was my sales team's most precious commodity. Russell was someone whom I had hired to run a new growth territory. He had great potential, the right experience, and the referral of some quality folks in our respective industry. I'll never forget the look on Russell's face when I explained my locked door analogy. I told him it was very simple: time was his most precious commodity, and the first six months would tell me if he believed that. Accordingly, selling was like being in a building with many locked doors. If you unlocked the right door, you'd find treasure; if the door didn't open, then you needed to be careful how long you took trying to open it. A door that doesn't open is more than likely locked, and if you don't have the key, you're wasting that precious time mentioned earlier.

Regrettably, Russell didn't believe me. He continued to try things that were not working. This unwillingness to pay heed to his time resulted in failure. He should have stopped and faced up to the fact that he didn't have the right keys to the doors before him. Though he never told me, I imagine he thought one more try would do it. He relied on past triumphs to get through present-day challenges. It didn't work, and Russell ignored reality to his own cost.

GOOD ADVICE

What value do you place on good advice? If you're like me, it's very important to have a key group of people there to advise and consult. This is especially important if you've decided life is meant to be lived well. You can't get there by yourself. People we place in our inner circle are key if we want that life we were called to. They give us perspective we could not gain on our own. They help us conquer our blind spots. Consequently, these folks will be able to see what we sometimes fail to.

As a caution, don't think that just anyone can fill the role of advisor. Far too many people seek advice from the wrong sources. I've mentioned in previous chapters that advisors and mentors should be those whom we trust. They must be people who are not impressed by us and are willing to tell us the truth. These criteria will shorten your list—that's a good thing. Your journey is far too important to leave to those who have an agenda or really don't care about your welfare.

The value in the right types of advisors is their ability to not only to be there, but to have a vested interest in our success. They are journeying through life with you. These advisors want to see you finish well, so give them your time and your most perplexing situations. By doing this, you will see what value these folks pour into your life.

My friend Harvey Hook is a shining example of what mentoring/ advising is all about. I sought Harvey out about five years ago to have breakfast. I was interested in his work and how it impacted the business community of Central Ohio.

Harvey and I met on a summer morning to get to know each other. I knew our meeting was divinely appointed. Harvey told me his story and how it shaped his view of life. I asked him if we could meet again, as I wanted to learn more. My gut made it clear I had found the right type of mentor.

The next series of meetings with Harvey would confirm the criteria for trust. His calm and affirming manner was tailored for my stormy ways of youth. So many times, as I struggled with my work situations, he would gently encourage and admonish. He wouldn't tell me what I wanted to hear, but he would make it clear that sometimes life is just tough. Talk about realistic thinking! I joked with Harvey later that he was converted into my mentor without knowing it.

There was one unexpected by-product of my relationship with Harvey, and that was his friendship. That may sound weird to you, but a deep friendship was not what I was looking for. Sometimes the unexpected is what can come from seeking help from another human being. I am proud to say Harvey is my mentor and my friend.

One of the greatest things Harvey did as a mentor was to exhort me to accept reality. He never advised me to stop dreaming or to embrace a safe path that others would feel good about. Harvey just encouraged me to remember that often reality is an opportunity disguised as a disappointment. We can only know this when we make a decision to accept reality. You can't manage what you haven't decided to do.

STARTING TODAY

What will you start today that will last a lifetime? You do realize life is often shaped by determinative decisions—small and large. We become what we choose to be. So here's an opportunity—make a decision today to embrace reality.

This may be a decision you think you've already made. However, can you remember the date and time of your decision? Do you recall the phase of life you were in? If these questions produce fog in your mind, then you probably never made the decision. The decision must be conscious and deliberate.

DECISION TIME

If you've taken my advice in this chapter, you'll start thinking about the next steps. First, you've evaluated where you are (what's working) in an honest way. Second, you've surrounded yourself with a few key advisors. Now is the time for building a habit through a decision. Don't fail to follow through here; a lot of what you want to become is rooted in how you make your decisions.

As I was heading into my late thirties, I met a wonderful man by the name of Rick Williams. We met by accident (or so I thought), and it changed my life. Even as wonderful as that was, I was challenged by Rick to make some key decisions around where I was heading. He made it clear that to live out anything of value would require a decision—a type of decision that revolved around discovering my destiny. Destiny journeys don't happen by osmosis. My search to find my destiny, thanks to making the decision, has been a watershed event.

For a moment, imagine if I would have allowed my appointed time to languish in indecision. Would I have grown? Would I have been willing to take key risks? No, I would have become like so many who allow their destinies to fade into memories of what could have been. I heard a quote once that said, "Fear regret more than failure." Those words are firmly implanted in my mind.

The art of life has eluded us. Making decisions relating to embracing reality is part of the art of life. Embracing reality begins today! The following are some helpful tips for becoming a better decision maker, connected directly to the embrace of reality:

- ✦ Start with a small decision, something easy, like reading to your child ten minutes a day for one week. After that, add something a little harder, like no sweet treats for two days. If you're wondering what's so determinative about my suggestions, think about the by-products of starting these small habits. In addition to improving your relationships and your health, you will be learning about building habits and creating a different way of life.

- ✦ Write down the decision you came up with in step 1. Don't be memory dependent. Writing it down will reinforce what you believe and give you perspective like nothing else.

- ✦ Go to your mentors. (I know after so many references to these role players in this book, you've got to have at least one.) Ask them for their opinions. Next, ask them to keep you accountable on seeing your decisions through.

- ✦ Ignore the critics! Every job, family, school, or church has critics. These are the people who feel it's their divine right to tell you what won't work. Never forget, critics are rarely remembered.

- ✦ Don't Give Up!

SECRET 7
Brand You

"Everybody writes his/her own life story. It is up to you to make it a legend or not."

--Author Unknown

A number of organizations, large and small, spend lots of time and effort building their specific brands. Some are even fanatical about protecting their brands' integrity. They painstakingly select just the right colors, the right fonts, and the right spokespeople to appear in ads for public consumption. To say millions of dollars are spent would be an understatement. The percentage of many a corporation's budget dedicated to branding might astound you. Why all the fuss? It's because these organizations know what impact their brand has on the bottom line.

So what about the individual brand? I'm referring to the one you and I carry with us all the time. We all have a brand to market, and we're making statements with it every day. Some brands are dead, some are dormant, and some are as bright as the sun. Some brands get attention, while others are ignored at the cost of the individual. No matter what your occupation, religion, or ethnic background, your brand is being shaped for the world to see.

Ever wonder how much money is spent on "brand you"? Millions? Thousands? The statistics say not much, if anything. Many experts say more than thirty percent of workers aren't engaged in their jobs. More than likely, a similar percentage of people are less than fully committed to life in general. More than a few of us wince at the idea of how we affect the world. We'd often rather leave affecting the world to Bono or Oprah. Though we might never be able to approach the renown of their good works, our brands were designed to have impact, too. Investing our hard-earned dollars to further our brand's influence seems to be an afterthought.

Just ask your co-workers and your boss about their personal brands. My gut says they'll look at you as if you have three heads, mostly because they don't know what their personal brands are. They get nervous just talking about it.

Branding is like religion; it shines a light on those things we'd rather ignore. Branding implies you'll look at what's right and what's wrong. It will ask a lot of you with no guarantee of return.

Imagine an investment guru asking you to invest in something that is great, but it's risky and lacking any proven return. Would you invest? Many great organizations started out taking this kind of risk when they put their brands in the marketplace. You're more important than the organization you work for—whether you know it or not. And your brand can make a greater impact on the world than theirs if you are brave enough to market it.

Do you see your personal brand as kind of murky and risky? You wouldn't be alone in those sentiments. Most people are afraid of so many things, so the idea of approaching their personal brand could be frightening. It could be so frightening they avoid their brand altogether. We've been duped into believing in the pain-free, no-cost approach to living. This approach keeps people from believing and investing in themselves because of the short-term pain associated with growing. Like the fifty-year-old male executive who decides to get in shape, with all his good intentions, so are we as we find out everything has a cost.

WHAT'S IN YOUR HEART?

Ludwig van Beethoven is quoted as saying, "I do not write for prestige or honor. What is in my heart must come out. That is why I compose." What if we lived out his statement? What if what is in our hearts is the key? What if our personal brand (brand you) is the thing we should be focusing on? It may not surprise you to know I'm sold out on Beethoven's statement! My quest is to assure that what is in my heart gets out. Care to join me?

When you reach the finish line, will you be measured by how much money you made or how long your title was? No, you will be measured by your legacy, which in many ways is your brand spread out for the entire world to see. There is nothing wrong with making lots of money along the way, and I am in favor of great success of all varieties. But success should be a by-product of living what is in your heart. And believe me, your heart is the best place to begin defining your brand. Your heart doesn't lie, it doesn't ignore, and it isn't looking for approval from the outside world. Oh, that we would listen to our hearts and have the life well lived.

One of the best examples of listening to the heart comes from my dear friend Clay Biggs. Clay is a fine musician (he plays the drums), and I've known him for almost twenty-five years. Music is what brought us together. Clay and I dreamed as teenagers we would play music for a living. Visions of fame and fortune danced in our heads. One thing was true of us as well, we were very insecure—insecure about how good we were and whether we could make it. Unfortunately, these insecurities (along with other pressures) choked out the desire to be living, active musicians. This was sad because we were wired to play and communicate through music.

Fast-forward, almost twenty years later, and Clay is playing again. He plays more than I can believe, but what is most inspiring and sweet is Clay's perspective. He now is secure! He's free from the burden of making it and free to pursue what is in his heart. Strange as it may seem, Clay is now better prepared to express his gift than when he was more energetic and goal oriented. This is not to say he lacks energy and goals. On the contrary, he has them…they're just new and more mature.

Now Clay is comfortable in his own skin. He knows who he is and what that means. How did he do it? Clay would tell you he is a work in progress. One event that had tremendous impact and defined a lot of what is occurring now was the death of Clay's father almost four years ago. Clay loved his father deeply, and the reality of his passing set Clay in place.

Though Clay has never told me directly, I believe he came to a point where time started to matter. A fact that is foreign to many. It is usually embraced by the dying or those who've lost deeply. Clay realizes he won't live forever and, while he has the energy, he must truly live. For Clay, part of truly living is playing music, his beautiful brand for all to hear.

So as you've discovered, the heart is a key component in unearthing and manifesting brand you. You have to stop holding your heart back because you fear you won't be a worldly success. Get the order right and you'll see the harmony. A key question is whether you and I are willing to take on the process of creation and living. It is not easy, and many ignore this path. If you plan to be truly successful, however, you'd better get comfortable with your heart and what's in it. The journey is worthy of your best.

WHY BOTHER WITH BRANDING?

You might be wondering why the topic of personal branding is rarely written about. I have a few theories, but the main one is the up-front pain. Like any endeavor to grow, there is up-front pain that will test your resolve. Consider this pain as a right of passage or entrance exam. Only the committed dare apply for personal branding. In twenty-first century America we don't like pain—short- or long-term. We've been convinced it's not necessary to sacrifice or endure challenging circumstances.

Think about it; you could confuse this book with an easy fix or anecdote. You could view it as a quick read I wrote to cure my felt needs. I've purposefully tried to make sure this book doesn't do the work for you. This book is a field guide for your journey; it does not make the journey for you. If I tried to tell you exactly what to do, it would be a futile exercise. No two personal brands are the same. Therefore, your path of discovery should be one found by you alone. Isn't that great? It implies that your brand is special and worth the effort and pain.

Our microwave mentalities and give-it-to-me-now approaches are killing our resolve to take the time needed for personal discovery. The energy and focus needed to win the race in front of us, as well as races we've yet to face, is lacking today. We're distracted and worn out by too much information, too much television, and too many self-serving endeavors. Given the state of our affairs, I can understand why few would even think about their own personal brand.

The only resolve that seems to stick is our rush to get on with the next chase. We're constantly lured by another thing, person, or adventure to try. We run, we catch, and we're left unsatisfied. And so it goes…like an endless treadmill.

ALL ABOUT THE MACHINE

So how does your employer fit in with the concept of brand you? Some courageous and dynamic organizations are working this idea of personal branding, but these enterprises are the exception, not the rule. If you happen to be working for one, be thankful. Please don't misunderstand, however, the organization is not responsible for your personal brand, you are.

Most organizations are too entranced by up-front rewards and successes to invest in growing their employees. They don't see an immediate return, so they place the idea of staff personal development in the we'll-table-that-for-the-next-quarter box. Sadly, they miss a great opportunity to increase profit and build loyalty within the enterprise.

Profit is good, but only when it is held in context. (Peter Drucker wrote some insightful thoughts about this in his classic *The Effective Executive.* His prediction that we would one day become a corporate society dominated by "knowledge workers" is now a reality.) That context here is development of people. When profit rules, you usually are just dealing with greed. Greed left unchecked is like letting a lion out of its cage. The bars are there for a reason, so organizations need to use them to keep profit in proper perspective.

Unfortunately, more organizations than not have left a vacuum that has not been properly filled. In meetings, we have talking points about how important employees, customers, and shareholders are. But then you read about people like Bob Nardelli, the CEO of Home Depot, leaving the company with a $200 million dollar retirement package. What was that board thinking when it signed that type of contract? Something has moved us over to hypocrisy.

CHOOSING NOT TO CHOOSE

Like organizations, individuals have choice in the matter of whether to market their brands. Today, however, many of us seem to have failed to exercise that choice. Perhaps we're too busy running to or from something we really can't describe to realize we've ignored this critical part of our personal development. We use rapid evaluations, quick fixes, and the easy road to delude ourselves into believing we are successful. It will be our great regret one day when we realize we've failed to take the time needed to achieve true success and find we lack the strength to face great odds. Our decision to ignore may produce a number of consequences, including the following:

+ We turn away from those most in need because we feel unable to offer a solution.

+ We fail to address a future unseen (vision).

+ We become unable to handle crisis. (Who we are is revealed in crisis.)

If you're not careful, your brand will be left in the hands of others. Remember, most organizations value conformity and duplication. If you leave your brand in the hands of your organization, your unique voice will become part of the annual report—a number and maybe a face, but no soul. Oh sure, they'll use romantic words designed to keep you interested by telling you authority is a tool to make decisions. But what would they say if you told them your work role needed to support your vision for a life well lived? How would they react if you wanted to explore an idea that was genuinely risky? You fill in the blank here; my gut says they'll want to move you back into their neat little mold.

You may make a lot of money, you may have a corner office, and you may have many who call you boss, but you will be defined by the organization. As we know, organizations can and do say goodbye. What then? Please remember that your brand is no accident. You have a brand whether you like it or not. Don't allow it to become the choice you never made. Don't allow it to be swallowed up by a culture of cynicism. Do the thinking; is your brand owned by you or someone/something else? The answer to that question is critical.

AS ONE THINKS

A long time ago, it occurred to me that life is played out in the realm of our thinking. Our thought life has been compared to a battleground, and I agree with that comparison. How we think—how our mental battles are won or lost—determines, to a large degree, what we will become. So as we tackle the how of personal branding, keep in mind the role your thoughts play in the way you market yourself. You can't execute on something that hasn't been settled in your mind. You can't exorcise all those demons of your past until your mind agrees.

MONEY, MONEY, MONEY

It's time to settle the issue of money. Money can be your master or your subject. In the area of personal branding, the latter is what you want. Why is money important? Money matters because we spend so much of our lives pursuing, amassing, fretting about, and obsessing over it.

Rich and poor follow the nasty money path, which interferes with living out the authentic self. A personal brand without authenticity is corrupt and shallow. Money needs a rightful place and perspective in what you do.

Let's now pay careful attention to what we do to survive versus what we do to live brilliantly. Earning money is a necessity for most; therefore, look at money for what it is. It is not a tool for finding happiness, fulfillment, or true love.

I've made the mistake of thinking money would do those things. When I was in Corporate America, continually striving to earn more money was almost habit forming. I found people treated me differently based on their perception of how much I made. The more successful I was, the more scrutiny and curiosity I faced.

I was retired early in one organization—a polite way of saying I was asked to leave. This was a painful and stressful time to be sure. I found myself with no corner office, no expense account, and no more direct reports. One thing stuck out during that time: only a few wanted to be as engaged with me as they were when I had a title, money, and the smell of success.

One of the few people who still sought me out was Jim Kaminski. His constant encouragement and advice filled me with hope, especially when I wasn't sure everything would go as planned. You need to understand, Jim is a very successful and sought-after leader. If he forgot me, nobody would complain or protest. But there he stood, not needing the trappings (money denominated) of a successful corporate career. Everyone needs a Jim, for such a person is valuable in so many ways.

So are you confusing the issue? Are you confusing your net worth with your self-worth? Ladies and gentlemen, money is a tool, so use it as such. When you're able to see it for what it is, you'll be able to focus on what personal branding is all about—the you who is (figuratively) naked for the world to see. You'll begin to see from a perspective that orders things around who you are, not what you are. In many ways, you'll possess a certain type of freedom. Money will become the slave it was meant to be. You need to keep in mind the human potential for greed and various insecurities, which can render you ineffective. If you hold these culprits in check, however, you'll see your brand and life flourish.

A LITTLE SELF- EXAMINATION

An examination of who you are is key in establishing your personal brand. You need to evaluate your journey and where you think you've landed so far. In many ways, this would be a good time to review the previous chapters. Look over the following chapter titles and reflect on what they've said to you:

+ Chapter 1, "Be Authentic"

+ Chapter 2, "Live a Life of Influence"

+ Chapter 3, "Don't Chase Success"

+ Chapter 4, "Beware of the Evil Number Seventeen"

+ Chapter 5, "Watercooler Conversations"

+ Chapter 6, "Embrace Reality"

As you evaluate where you are, consider that this is a process. Your journey or quest will be over a lifetime. Don't be too hard on yourself if you feel like you should be further along, and above all don't compare yourself to anyone else. That's a sure way to falter.

Do you like the results of the examination? Is there anything to change? If you're like most, there are many things to consider. I've found the most important things in your life are the ones to have in order. Can you name your top five priorities? Do they have your full allegiance and focus? They must if you want to be epic in all you do.

Everything we do is part of the design to have an epic life. What is an epic life? It is a life that matters and looks the way God made it to be. We're creating epic lives for ourselves whether we know it or not. A man wants to command his own ship because he believes that will deliver satisfaction. A woman wants to solve the AIDS crisis in Africa because she believes that will grant her significance. Even the poor souls who think owning expensive cars will define them do it to fill a void.

There are very few who wake up and say, "I want to be mediocre." Most wake up and hope they matter. They hope they matter to their spouses, their co-workers, and hopefully, God. What will be revealing is the steps or actions they will take to gain this acceptance. In the end, checking your motivations with the question *why* tells you a lot about the road you're on.

THE LOOKING BACK

If you were on an elevator with Nelson Mandela and he asked you to tell him your story, could you? Can you articulate a compelling portrait of your brand in the short time it takes to climb a few floors? What are you for? What do you want your legacy to be? I'm going to take you on the journey to answer those questions and then discuss how to market your brand with simplicity.

One of the toughest things for most people to do is look back. Painful memories of failed marriages, death, job loss, or hurtful words fill their minds. These memories can neutralize you quickly. If you have the courage, stay with me. Answer the following question: could that pain or hurt be something that has made you better or helped you grow? You must accept all of life as a gift—the type of gift given to help you become more than you imagined you could be.

Consider the following and see if you find any common ground with me:

+ Death of a loving grandmother

+ Incarceration of a brother

+ Diagnosis of Type I diabetes

+ Loss of a child

+ Betrayal

+ Careerism

+ Corporate Downsizing

See, you and I are alike in more ways than you thought. Many fall into the trap of thinking they're all alone. As I've pointed out, nothing could be further from the truth. The question we need to ask then is what effects those events and circumstances have had on our personal brands. Are you crippled by the memories? Are you bitter? Are you defeated? If the answer is yes to any of these questions, you need to look at the opportunity that lies underneath the pain. There is healing waiting for you there.

I've shared some of my deepest hurts, so pull out a piece of paper and write down your experiences. Be sure to capture them all. Don't just write down the painful ones, but write the happy ones as well. All experiences, happy and sad, play a part in defining us. Next, order your experiences by approximate dates. The dates will help you create a story time line. Seeing your life as a story will illuminate your path with clarity.

Now read your story aloud. This is your core brand. Are you willing to talk about it? Are you willing to share it with the world? You can try to hide it, but everyone's brand is exposed.

If a man is a jerk to his wife, everyone can see it. They may not realize his behavior is a reflection of how his dad treated his mom, but the behavior itself is still evident for all to see. If the man isn't conscious of his brand, he won't do anything to change it. He'll forever be marked as an example of someone people could explain but never excuse. The greater outcome would be for the man to humbly look at what's causing his abusive behavior and make a decision to change for the better.

Why not be in charge of communicating your brand instead of giving out a message you're not conscious of. Words can speak life or death to the hearer, so choose wisely.

SINCERE MESSAGING

As you come to grips with your message, make sure you can speak to it with sincerity. Ask yourself what you've learned from your experiences. How have you changed? How has living through your ups and downs allowed you to help someone? If you can't think of anything, then start a new story. Start a story of volunteering at a battered women's shelter. Start a story of helping someone you know change career paths. There is no better way to breathe life into something than getting out there and doing it.

Don't blurt out your story just as you brainstormed it. Think of it this way: if you were listening to a story, what would you want to hear? More than likely, you'd want to hear something inspiring or something positive. Well there you have it, be out there with the most inspiring and positive elements of your story. As you deliver your message (written or spoken), smile and be enthusiastic. Most people are frowning and appear to be uninspired because they fear the future. So why don't you choose to be part of a better future—one that includes those who are listening to and/or reading your story? Tell your story as you've envisioned it to be. Make it something people can root for.

In one of my first corporate speaking engagements, I was asked to address a small group about casting vision. To say I was excited would be putting it lightly. The session lasted for about an hour and fifteen minutes. One of the participants, Sarah, graciously allowed me to coach out her dreams. She wanted to be an English professor at Columbia University. She knew the road would be long, but it was obvious how much passion she had for the dream.

I defined vision as a preferable future, Sarah agreed, and we began. First, I asked her to spare no detail. I told her all the experiences in her mind should be fuel for the vision. She initially leapt to the Columbia classroom and the students she pictured teaching. Then I asked her to think of where she would live, what fall would be like in New York City, and the flavor of her favorite coffee. Sarah smiled. Never underestimate the power of the small details of life. We moved onto the vision around Columbia and the job. It was obvious she had more energy by the time we were through. She had a breakthrough because what she saw became life.

This story illustrates how powerful a personal brand can be. The vision Sarah articulated that day left many inspired, and in a significant way, she inspired herself as well. I don't know if Sarah ever got to Columbia. Getting there would certainly require a lot of hard work. But one thing's for sure, she left an imprint on my soul.

By the way, Sarah was a mid-level supervisor at a medium-sized company in Ohio. Everyone has a great story in them; it just depends on whether they are willing to tell the world about it.

YOUR CONSTITUTION

The Founding Fathers knew it was important to have a constitution outlining the principles that guide our nation. In the same way, it's important for you to have a written document outlining the principles that guide your life—your brand. Some call these vision statements; others call them mission statements. Whatever label you prefer is secondary. What's key is having a document you review regularly to serve as a reminder and as a tool to be refined over your lifetime.

Your constitution should explain the who, what, when, and why questions. Who am I? What do I want to be? When will I start? Why does this journey matter? Through the answers to these questions, your constitution should paint a life picture for the world around you.

Though your constitution doesn't grant power, it will unleash it. If you write it with sincerity, the document will be inspiring. If you write it for someone else, it will be shown as a fake. Remember to be who you are, God wrote a wonderful story in your heart. Trying to please people or playing for an audience you seek approval from is a dead-end street.

THE CRAFT OF CRAFTING

You've already spoken your story into life, so crafting it into a written document won't be too difficult (easy for me to write). Seriously, take a look at the following excerpt from my constitution:

> *As it relates to Leadership, God intends for me to lead those who are in my sphere of influence. I will encourage, develop, and exhort people of diverse backgrounds. The marketplace is the arena in which He desires me to have influence. I see myself expanding that influence through speaking*

engagements, teaching, and one-to-one mentoring. I also see Epic Living as the organization focused on developing and reproducing people of influence within the public and private sector.

That excerpt comes from the vision section of my document. It reflects my best understanding of what God is painting on the canvas of my life. Trust me, I didn't just wake up one day and pound that statement out. I did it the way I've advised you to do: speak your story into life to yourself and then share it with the world around you. After many recitations, it will become a part of you.

You will discover as you write and live out your constitution that change is a process and not an event. Give yourself the room needed to see you're in a marathon and not a sprint.

Don't beat yourself up over the need for edits and re-dos. They are inevitable and healthy. My first draft was choppy and, I might add, full of fear. The fear came from writing such an important document. But I had a mentor who encouraged me every step of the way.

IN THE END

What action will you take to ensure you don't make the graveyard rich? It's true; we will either make the graveyard rich or poor. I once heard Dr. Myles Munroe relay a story around this. He said the richest place in all the world is not the oil fields of Saudi Arabia or the diamond mines of South Africa. It is the graveyard, for the graveyard is the place where all the "I love yous" and the love affairs never started are kept. The graveyard also holds all the businesses never started and the books never written (almost me).

As Dr. Munroe alluded, we were intended to leave the grave poor. It should be destitute because the dreams were lived and manifested. Sadly, the statistics are not in our favor. Most of us have failed to realize the importance of life, let alone our personal brands. Many have been duped into believing they don't matter. It's a boss who rarely makes eye contact, a spouse too busy to listen, or voices from the past that all conspire to bring us low. It is a tragic reality for a life to waste away. It is also a tragedy to sit and watch it happen.

We've decided to let others live out our stories. Brad Pitt looks like the part we would have played. Senator Barak Obama can rally people the way we wish we could. Why not just let them do it? Ladies and gentlemen, those folks are imposters. Not in their own stories, but in yours. No one was given your personal brand other than you.

So will we see and hear your story soon?

Acknowledgements

A chapter would not be enough space to cover all the people who've helped me in the process of writing my first book. I'm sure I've forgotten someone or something, but here is my best attempt at saying thank you to the following:

+ My Heavenly Father for loving me so much that He would write a story called my life.

+ My wife, Eileen, for loving me as no other could. She was sent from heaven to me, and I've never been the same since.

+ Lauren and Grant for blessing me without knowing it.

+ My parents for unwavering support and love.

+ My mentors Rick Williams and Harvey Hook for loving me, encouraging me, advising me, pointing me to God, and putting up with me when times were tough.

+ Larcel McGhee for being a "divine appointment" who changed my life.

+ Juanell Teague who came from out of nowhere to encourage and teach me.

+ Jon Hanson for mentoring me at just the right time.

+ Steve Hopkins for encouraging me at opportune times.

+ Jim Kaminski for caring when many didn't.

+ My editor, Deb Boerema, for making sense of my writing.

+ Sarah Naess for her valuable proof reading.

+ Brent Long of Long on Life for kindness and
  encouragement.

+ To all those touched by my writing, living, or speaking—
  the feeling is mutual.